THIRD PERSON RURAL

Noel Perrin, teacher, writer, and farmer (in that order), was city-born but country-bred. Now living in Thetford, Vermont (reputedly the last operating theocracy in America), he teaches at Dartmouth College and scours a precarious living from the flinty New England soil. His articles, reviews, and hints on animal (and human) husbandry in sources as diverse as *Country Journal* and *The New York Times Book Review* have delighted audiences nationwide. Unawed by his fame, Mr. Perrin continues to devote his time to understanding the fickle ways of nature and the feckless behavior of non-natives. His books include *Giving Up the Gun: Japan's Reversion to the Sword, 1543–1879*, *First Person Rural*, and *Second Person Rural*, the latter two of which are also available in Penguin Books.

THIRD PERSON RURAL

Further Essays of
a Sometime Farmer

BY NOEL PERRIN

PENGUIN BOOKS

PENGUIN BOOKS
Viking Penguin Inc., 40 West 23rd Street,
New York, New York 10010, U.S.A.
Penguin Books Ltd, Harmondsworth,
Middlesex, England
Penguin Books Australia Ltd, Ringwood,
Victoria, Australia
Penguin Books Canada Limited, 2801 John Street,
Markham, Ontario, Canada L3R 1B4
Penguin Books (N.Z.) Ltd, 182–190 Wairau Road,
Auckland 10, New Zealand

First published in the United States of America by
David R. Godine, Publisher, Inc., 1983
Published in Penguin Books 1985

Acknowledgments: "Winter Escape," "A One-Horsepower Mower," and "On
Porcupine Hill" are reprinted by permission of *Vermont Life.* "Man of a Thou-
sand Odors" is reprinted by permission of *The New York Times.* "Two Letters
to Los Angeles" is reprinted by permission of the *Los Angeles Times.* "The
Gourmet Potato Grower" and "Farm Flowers" are reprinted by permission of
Horticulture. "My Life as a Peasant" is reprinted by permission of *Boston.*
"Birth in the Pasture" and "How to Farm Badly" are reprinted by permission of
Country Journal. "Class Struggle in the Woods" is reprinted by permission of
Sportscape. "Low Technology in the Sugarbush" is reprinted by permission
of *U.S. Air Magazine.* "The Possibility Tax" and "Nuclear Disobedience" are
reprinted by permission of *Inquiry.* All appear here in revised form. *No Time
but Place,* quoted in "The Beef Cow's Plea to the Vegetarians," was published
by McGraw-Hill, Inc., in 1980. The lines quoted from "Two Tramps in Mud
Time" and "Build Soil" are reprinted by permission of the estate of Robert
Frost. They appear exactly as Mr. Frost wrote them.

Printed in the United States of America by
R. R. Donnelley & Sons Company, Harrisonburg, Virginia
Set in Janson

For Burnley Taylor Perrin,
whose own farm is small (as it would have
to be, being located on a rooftop in
Washington, D.C.) but exceptionally well run.

Foreword

THIS BOOK, like *First* and *Second Person Rural*, owes its existence in part to Walter Hard and Richard Ketchum.

Walter Hard was editor of *Vermont Life* from 1950 to 1972. When I first met him in 1961, I had been living in rural Vermont for one year. I still supposed myself to be an urbane writer, if no longer an urban one. I had plenty to say about Clos de Vougeot, absolutely nothing to say about cows. When Walter got through with me, I still had nothing to say about cows—but I was writing freely about cider and maple syrup. And I had discovered that it was almost as much pleasure to write about these things as it was to press the one and boil the other.

Richard Ketchum was one of the two founders of *Country Journal* in 1974. It was originally called *Blair & Ketchum's Country Journal*. Blair ran the business side and Ketchum the editorial side; they still do. They just don't sound like partners in a nineteenth-century patent medicine business any more. I met Dick in 1973, when he was struggling to get the magazine started, and I was struggling to move from being a play-farmer to being a part-time real farmer. Before I quite realized what was happening, he had me writing about beef cows in *Country Journal*—and it has been all downhill from there. In 1961 when I went back to New

York on a visit, I used to enjoy pretending to be a hick; some years ago I realized there was no longer any pretense involved.

There is a limit to how much blame Hard and Ketchum can be expected to take, however. *Third Person Rural* is the last book of mine they will bear any responsibility for. I may write a few more rural essays—in fact, I know for certain I'll write at least one more. There's a little corner of my back pasture that visitors sometimes think is a pet graveyard, because there is row after row of posts set close together in the ground. It's actually three of every kind of tree that grows on the place. I wanted systematic information on what kind of fence posts last longest, and I already have five years' worth of data. The expected, such as that basswood keels right over; the unexpected, such as that white birch doesn't. In five more years I foresee an article.

But there will not be any *Fourth Person Rural*. Three is enough.

About *Third Person Rural* there is one thing to explain. The pieces in it are both new and old. The twelve linked essays called "A Country Calendar" are old. They originally appeared, in somewhat different form, in a picture book called *Vermont in All Weathers*, published in 1973 and long out of print. The others are mostly quite recent.

A lot can change in ten years, both on a farm and in a life. One horse is sold, another bought. Small daughters turn into college students. A place with six acres of fenced pasture becomes a place with thirty-two acres of fenced pasture. A married author abruptly turns single. Probably not all the inconsistencies in this book are explained by the ten-year span, but most of them are.

NOEL PERRIN
March, 1983

Contents

Contents

Part 1

A Country Calendar

JANUARY

During three months in the year, this part of America is covered with snow.

The Rev. Dr. Samuel Williams,
The Natural and Civil History of Vermont, 1794.

EITHER THE CLIMATE HAS CHANGED a lot in the last hundred and ninety years, or Dr. Williams was an incorrigible optimist. Four and a half months is more like it, and sometimes it's five. There is an awful lot of snow. I think of the winter my elder daughter was ten. It started with a blizzard on November twenty-fifth. We had a white Thanksgiving, marked by many missing guests. Then a white Christmas, a white Valentine's Day, and a white Easter. The snow was just beginning to go from the fields —not yet from the woods—the week after Easter, when another big storm came sliding in. It restored a foot of snow to open ground and built the level in the woods back up to a full three feet. I got my truck stuck in a snowdrift

on April fourteenth. There was no bare ground worth
mentioning until April twentieth. Five months winter
lasted.

Of all this time, January is the supreme snow month.
I'm not saying the most snow falls then, because it doesn't.
In January it's usually too cold to snow as much as it does
in, say, March. But the snow and the biting cold dominate
life in a way they do at no other time.

They even dominate aesthetically. January is the month
of blue shadows. Whether it's the lowness of the sun, or
the purity of the air (no pollen, no dust now), the unsullied
whiteness of the snow, or merely some kind of reflection
from the bright January sky, I have no idea. But in January
when the sun puts the shadow of a line of trees across a
snowy field, the shadow is a blue-gray to be seen in no
other circumstances. It is almost worth being that cold to
go out to look at shadows. Late afternoon—that is, three to
four o'clock; it's going to be dark before five—is the best
time.

Except for shadow-watching, there are fairly few out-
door amusements in Vermont in January. Downhill skiers
are out, and snowmobilers go snowmobiling, usually in
small herds of six to ten. You often hear them at bedtime.
Like deer and rabbits, snowmobilers are considerably noc-
turnal; and like other native species they have developed a
special winter coat that keeps them warm on even the cold-
est nights.

Small children occasionally get a certain pleasure out of
squeaking. This they can do simply by walking around
outside any time the temperature drops to ten above or
colder. The snow squeaks at each step.

Grown-ups occasionally get a certain pleasure out of taking a maul and splitting a big elm log, especially one they have previously tried splitting in the summer. Elm is a cross-grained wood, and most of the year a really large elm log is hard or even impossible to split in two by hand. You have to keep working around the perimeter, like a veneer machine, or one person making a double bed. But now the sap is frozen, and one well-placed blow in the heartwood will often cause even a two-foot elm log to shiver apart. Better use a good splitting maul, though. When it's that cold, badly tempered steel sometimes shivers, too.

Most Januaries there is a period of five or ten days when nonstop squeaking would be possible and when everything shivers. The temperature drops to twenty or thirty below every night and climbs to perhaps two above at the warmest instant of the day. If there is also a wind blowing, anyone except a snowmobiler in his special suit or a fanatic skier wearing a face mask can comfortably be outdoors for approximately ten minutes. Hairy and downy woodpeckers, who have to be out all the time, need special attention now. Frozen grubs just won't keep them going; they crave an Eskimo diet. I have seen a handful of small woodpeckers go through a pound of pork fat in one day.

Machinery is also hard to keep going, and a large number of decisions to buy a new car is made annually during this period. The first morning that your car won't start, you are angry. The second, you are furious. Also late to work, since the man who owns the garage has eight other cars to start before he can get to yours. That night you decide to take your battery out and keep it in the house until morning. But your hands get so cold trying to loosen the terminals that you compromise by leaving it in the car and putting an old blanket over the hood. You also go out at bedtime and let the engine run for ten minutes, guilt or no guilt. When it doesn't start the third morning, you are fair game for the dealer.

For the handful of people who still keep driving horses, however, the January cold spell is a moment of glory. A neighbor of mine is fond of telling of a January morning that was cold even beyond the usual for cold spells. Along with a crowd of other men, he was down at the store in South Strafford, waiting to use the tractor starter. While he was waiting, an old fellow came driving up in a horse and buggy, looking insufferably smug. (You were expecting a sleigh? No one can use sleighs since we started salting the roads.)

"I knowed him," my neighbor says, "so I said, 'Morning, Earl! How cold was it up to your place?' The old fellow gave his horse a flick. 'Dunno. Thermometer only goes down to minus forty.' He looked the crowd of men over carelessly and added, 'Hoss don't care, anyway.' "

I myself knew a Vermont girl of twenty, who did house-cleaning and babysitting one winter for the family of a Dartmouth professor. It gets just as cold across the river in New Hampshire. Doreen had a fifteen-year-old Dodge she drove to work. When she appeared right on time the fourth morning in a row of January cold spell—a morning, as it happens, that her employer was waiting impatiently for the garageman to come start his new station wagon—he broke down and asked her what her trick was. No trick at all. "Daddy just hitches up the team," she said, "and drags me till it starts."

January is not all cold and snow. Along toward the end of the month comes a myth known as the January thaw. It is not entirely a myth, either. One terrible year there was a period of three days in late January when the temperature never went below freezing, and it hardly ever stopped raining. Cold is bad; cold and wet is worse.

Even more disagreeable, there was once a January thirty-first when, just before noon, the temperature on the front porch of my farmhouse went up to fifty-six. Later that day I went up to thirty. Feet, that is. On a ladder. Onto the roof to chop ice. Once a foot or so of snow has built up on the roof of the house, it begins to melt a little on the underside, from the heat of even a well-insulated house. A little water trickles quietly down under the snow to the eaves, where it promptly freezes again. By the time of January thaw an ice dam six or eight inches high may have built up. What with the rain and the thawing weather, a good-sized lake now forms behind it. Presently a stream of water comes coursing down the wallpaper in the front hall. It is time to chop ice, and I do. Just for a minute I consider selling the farm as well as the car and moving to Arizona.

F E B R U A R Y

The severest cold of our winters never kills any of our young trees, and seldom freezes any of our young cattle, although they are not housed during the winter. Nor is the cold so affecting to the human body, as the extremes and sudden changes from heat to cold on the seacoast.

Samuel Williams, 1794.

CONSIDERING THAT I HAVE HAD three successive sets of young pear trees winter-killed, I cannot wholly

7

agree with this claim, either. But Dr. Williams is certainly right about cattle and people. We get through winters fine. It may have been a little chilly during the January cold spell, and if there was also a January thaw, the slush was horrible. But the rest of winter is quite bearable, and especially February is.

In February the days are longer, the sun is higher, and the snow is more dramatic. Sometimes it is downright stagy. An evening flurry will come down in huge wet flakes, so thick and fast that you think in an hour the village will be buried like Pompeii. But the flurry stops in ten minutes, leaving two inches of perfect snowball snow, the first since Christmas. More often there will be a drifting snow of big feathery flakes. Floating down at midnight past the streetlight at the east end of the covered bridge in Thetford Center, the flakes seem both something holy, and too much and too beautiful, as if there were a Broadway stage crew dropping them from a helicopter a hundred feet up.

The morning after such a snow is what gave rise to picture postcards in the first place. The sky is clear. The air is still and cold, but not too cold. The snow doesn't squeak. From every chimney in the village a thick plume of smoke is rising straight upward. Every tree branch and even every strand of barbed wire has its snow tracery. When you drive to work (your car roaring easily to life, even though you didn't get a new one, after all), you pass through a little valley with an unfrozen brook running through it. The brook is sending up so much vapor into the fifteen-degree air that for fifty yards on either side the branches, the barbed wire, the very weeds (where they are tall and come up through the snow) are mere vehicles for crystals and complicated jewelry of ice.

8

Later in the day it's likely to be good weather for children to make snowmen and snow forts. In January it was too cold, and the snow wouldn't pack. Now it gets above freezing for several hours most days. Occasionally there is even a day that stirs the trees. I remember a February second that just plain woke them up. I was putting up new fence to enlarge a pasture. Should have done it in the fall, but hadn't. No one drives fence posts in February, and I was stringing wire along a section of old stone wall where I could be a sloven and fasten it to the trees.

About halfway I came to a fair-sized sugar maple. I had the wire pretty tight, and the first staple I tried to drive went part way in and then pulled out again. Immediately a gush of sap poured out the two little holes, as if the tree were bleeding from a snakebite. One could have made syrup that day.

By no means all February days are like that. There was one last year, and near the end of the month, too, when it was twenty-nine below when I got up. The pipes in the kitchen were frozen solid, the pigs were buried under straw in their pighouse, and though they came charging out for breakfast, the last of their slops froze in the trough before they could gulp them down.

But mostly there is some mildness in the air. And because so much of Vermont is steep hillsides, the reviving sun is able to melt snow on south cants even while it remains three feet deep on level ground and four feet or more on northern slopes. The beef cattle were able to do a little grazing around the bases of trees growing on south slopes even on that day that started at twenty-nine below. Seldom except during an actual blizzard do they even bother to go into the three-sided shelter (open to the south, of course) that I built just below the spring in their pasture. Just as Dr. Williams said, they like to be out.

I am out a good deal myself now. February days are wonderful for walking in the woods. I used to do it mostly on snowshoes, but since the advent of the snowmobile, I walk on snowmobile trails. Once I was following one up Jackson Brook and came on what I can only describe as a deer highway, crossing the snowmobile trail at right angles. It was a well-trodden path about eight inches wide (two-lane for deer). Even sharply marked by color, because so many oak and beech leaves had drifted onto it. A tan-brown highway through the white snow. I turned right and followed it, and in about a mile came to a deeryard I had never known existed. Six deer were home when I got there—placid enough so that instead of exploding out in all directions when they smelled me, they left at a trot, single file, on another highway at the far side.

I wish Interstates 89 and 91 left as little mark on the land as those two highways had when I went back to see them in May.

MARCH

The weather is cold, and in general pretty uniformly so . . . until the beginning of March, when with much bois-terous weather there begin to appear some slight indica-tions of spring.

Zadock Thompson,
History of Vermont, 1842.

SLIGHT INDICATIONS, INDEED. They do not include green fields—the first small patches of green appear in pastures about mid-April—much less early flowers, or leaves on the trees. Both of these belong to May. In fact, spring is the wrong word altogether. As someone pointed out a few years ago, Vermont does not have four seasons, but six. First comes unlocking, then spring, summer, fall, locking, and finally winter. What begins in March is unlocking. Its enemies call it mud season, because what unlocks first is the ground, but that's not a fair name. There *is* considerable mud, but there is also much beauty of kinds never to be seen in warmer or drier climates.

Just as unlocking begins, there is one indication, so subtle and slight that it's easily missed. Every year one of the first four or five days in March is going to be warm and brilliantly sunny, with the temperature briefly rising to near sixty. If you look hard at a birch or a red maple that day, you seem to see a faint haze of color in the upper branches: yellow for a birch, and red, of course, for a red maple. Look again the next day, and it's gone. Nothing but bare dark branches, and probably a sleet storm. All the same, unlocking has begun.

Dirt roads, being the only ground not covered by snow, unlock first. Each warm day the top inch or two of road touched by the sun thaws out. The first car going by makes a couple of inch-deep ruts, which get frozen in that evening. The next warm day they thaw, and with the first car, deepen, until presently only four-wheel-drive vehicles, and sometimes only four-wheel-drive vehicles with chains, can get through. It is no accident that town meeting is timed to come just before the roads unlock. I myself live on a paved road, but I love dirt roads. Every year until I finally bought a four-wheel myself, I could count on getting stuck twice: once in March because I always think a truck will do more than it can; once in May because I can't believe that abandoned roads in the woods aren't dried out yet.

Rivers unlock next. The two I know best, the Connecticut and the Ompompanoosuc (called the Pompy by those who live along it), both start the same way. You see two small streams running on top of the ice, one near each frozen bank. Then one day toward the middle of March, a patch of open water appears. Then another. On the Connecticut, which has many dams and much slow water, these patches slowly enlarge for a week, until one day you notice an open channel with a line of ice floes sailing solemnly down the middle.

The Pompy is more dramatic. The whole lower stretch usually opens in a single day. On the morning of that day, drive along Vermont Highway 132. The winding road follows the bends of an ice-locked river with just two or three open pools. Suddenly you notice that at the downstream end of one of these pools there is a little ice jam—half a dozen floes tipped up and piled on each other. These are partially blocking the current and building up pressure. The river has made itself a key.

Come back in two hours, and the jam is now very much bigger and half a mile lower. A surprisingly neat channel stretches away behind it. Even as you watch, the solid ice in front of the jam buckles and breaks, and the whole jam surges ahead. Another twenty feet of river are unlocked. Two more hours, and the Pompy has smashed and broken itself a channel right down to where it flows into the Connecticut. A whole flotilla of ice rides out into the bigger river and begins the silent trip south. A few more days, and the Dartmouth crews will be out practicing on the Connecticut, their eight-oared shells dodging the occasional twenty-foot piece of ice that still comes sailing down from Bradford. The river is not muddy, and not very high: white-water time is yet to come.

Meanwhile, two other kinds of unlocking have been taking place. Town meeting marks the resumption of social life. It never wholly ceased during the winter, but between the cold and the darkness, it slowed down considerably. Now, at what is the real beginning of the year, most of the town gathers to plan the year's business.

Scale is everything. If the million or so voters in Los Angeles were to gather in one place, you would have at worst a mob and at best a mass audience. But when eighty or so voters in West Fairlee or several hundred in Thetford gather, you have what feels remarkably like a true operation of democracy. Not on all issues—the states and the federal government have some very effective locking devices, using money and law both—but on enough to count.

I felt this most intensely at Thetford town meeting a few years ago. We met as usual in the gymnasium at the Academy, at 10:00 A.M. on the first Tuesday after the first Monday in March. The three selectmen, the town clerk, and the moderator of town meeting were up front. The rest of us—only about a hundred and fifty back then—were in folding chairs on the basketball court. Several women from Post Mills, the village whose turn it was to provide lunch that year, were in the back heating casseroles and cutting up pies, occupations that didn't keep them out of either the discussion or the voting.

We had seventeen articles to vote on, all previously announced in the town warning. Most of them were pretty small potatoes, such as Article 8: "To see if the Town will appropriate a sum of money, not to exceed $200, for Thetford Volunteer Fire Department." (We did.) But Article 12 was the biggest potato in four or five years. It concerned the covered bridge in Thetford Center, one of the two left in town. (There were once six. Two perished of neglect long ago; two were dismantled by the Army Engineers when they built a flood control dam in 1952. Pity we have no floods to control.)

The Thetford Center bridge was too small for big trucks to go through. It was also badly in need of repair. The selectmen and the one businessman in town who operates big trucks wanted to tear it down and put up a modern concrete highway bridge. Most people thought they would succeed.

We got through the first eleven articles in less than an hour. Then we spent the rest of the morning arguing—"debating" is too lofty a term for town meeting style—Article 12. Sentiment gradually mounted for keeping the covered bridge, chiefly because of the brilliant fight put up by an old man who had been our rural mail carrier for fifty-one years—had taken the mail through that bridge in a horse and sleigh, then a 1911 Cadillac, and finally a Jeep station wagon. It came near time to vote. Then one of the proponents of the new bridge got up, holding a formidable list in his hand. He told us he liked the old wooden bridge as well as anyone—but he wasn't sure we realized how much it would cost to repair it. And he began reading specifications and prices from his list: the number of new twelve-by-twelve bridge timbers required and what each would cost; numbers and prices for joists; and so on. The total kept mounting; we taxpayers began having second thoughts.

Then a young fellow in back stood up, a workingman with a lumberjack's shirt on and a three-day growth of beard. "I don't know where he got them prices from," he said, "but I know this. I work up to the mill in Ely, and we can sell you all that stuff a hell of a lot cheaper than what he said." Every head turned to stare. Undeterred, he went from memory through each item the other man had mentioned, repeating the figures and then quoting the lower price his mill could offer.

After that we voted. Usually we have voice votes to save time, but this was an important decision, and the selectmen passed out slips of paper. We wrote "Yes" if we wanted a new bridge, "No" if we didn't. We filed by the ballot box and dropped the slips in, and, when we finished, the selectmen counted them. It took fifteen minutes. The First Selectman then walked to the microphone. "Guess we're keepin' it," he said. "Twenty-one 'Yes,' hundred and twenty-one 'No.'" There was a brief roar of triumph. Then we had lunch.

The other March unlocking is done with a brace and bit, and it consists of tapping the maples. But unlocking, alias mud time, alias sugar season, continues from March into April, and I shall save it for then.

APRIL

You know how it is with an April day
When the sun is out and the wind is still,
You're one month on in the middle of May.
But if you so much as dare to speak,
A cloud comes over the sunlit arch,

THIRD PERSON RURAL

A wind comes off a frozen peak,
And you're two months back in the
middle of March.

Robert Frost, *"Two Tramps in Mud Time."*

THE RURAL CHARACTER IS FORMED more in April than at any other time of year. At least it is around here. By "the rural character" I mean a combination of wariness, stoicism, and unruffled acceptance of things as they are that is quite different from the usual urban character. You might say that most city people believe that all problems (except maybe those caused by their neighbors) are in the end soluble, while most country people know better. Naturally the weather has a lot to do with why.

In cities—in New York, for example—any intrusion of the weather is regarded as a kind of affront. If it rains at 5:00 P.M., people don't actually hold the mayor responsible, but they do stand under their umbrellas waiting in some indignation for taxis. Their shoes were not designed for rain; why has someone not put a dome over the city?

If it rains very hard and there is flooding—if, say, the Sixth Avenue Subway is delayed by water on the tracks—people do indeed hold the city responsible. Delays are unnatural and intolerable. A cure must be found, just as summer has been cured by air conditioning, and mud season by paving most of the city.

There is no cure for Vermont weather. It is consistent only in its inconsistency. (Once during a drought there was a half-hour's hard rain on the back of my farm; not a drop fell on the house and garden.) April is the most inconsistent of all. If anything, Frost understates the case. Here is a sequence, for example, from a year when I was keeping unusually close track of things:

April 3: So hot in the morning that my small daughters were out playing bare to the waist, and day lily shoots appeared. It turned abruptly cold at 3:00 P.M., and there were gusts of snow.

April 4: Twenty-four degrees at breakfast time. Cold all day.

April 5: Almost hot. Under a powerful sun, nearly all remaining snowdrifts melted from fields.

April 6: Mild, cloudy—and snowing. Two inches of snow fell, and stuck. The result was a very beautiful afternoon. All small ponds had melted and were open water, now surrounded by, and reflecting, snow-covered grass and bushes.

April 7: Rain and sleet from dawn until 9:00 A.M.—the roads glazed with ice—driving terrible. It then turned to snow, and five inches of wet flakes came pelting down. Trees bent worse than any time this winter. If I weren't so worried about losing a lot of them, I would think their poses beautiful.

April 8: Sunny and warm. The trees erect by noon, but the fields remain snow-covered.

There is no rational way to deal with a stretch of weather like this. If you wake up to an April snow, you have to go on and shovel—and the town has to plow a hundred miles or so of roads—even though you know perfectly well that by noon it may be a hot day and the snow will melt by itself. Right now it's 7:00 A.M., and people have to get to work. Besides, it may equally well turn cold and snow twice as hard in the afternoon. Optimists lose every time in a Vermont April.

This is not to say there are no pleasures in the month. On the contrary, starting about April tenth there is an endless string of them, as unlocking turns to spring. First the pussy willows come out and the rivers run emerald green. Then the deer come out. Mid-April is the best time of the whole year for watching deer. After a winter of eating tree-buds, and not too many of them, they are mad for grass. They come boldly into the fields to eat last year's withered stems. One morning this past April I saw nine deer in the pasture behind my house.

A few days later the robins arrive, sometimes in flocks of two or three hundred, brightening the bare, brown southern hillsides. About the same time, spring peepers start up. Then fields begin to green. For some reason, the green always appears first where the snow has melted last. Roughly one day after the green tips appear, the first woodchuck pops up. Woodchucks are great gourmets, and they are not about to eat old winter-killed hay, as the deer do. In the April sun their brown fur has red glints in it; for a couple of weeks, until the grass gets long or a neighbor boy appears with a .22, they make nice accent marks in the fields.

But the greatest April pleasure is sugaring. Back in Dr. Williams's time, two-thirds of the families in the state (his estimate) spent part of the month gathering sap and boiling. Even now I'd guess a third of rural families do.

Sugaring usually begins in mid-March and runs until mid-April. These dates are anything but fixed, however, the weather being what it is. This past spring the first good run in Thetford didn't come until almost the end of March (we were having sub-zero mornings almost up to St. Patrick's Day), and most of us closed down around April twenty-fourth. A few diehards kept boiling until the first of May.

One joy of sugaring is that you take advantage of the inconstant weather. In fact, the more capricious the weather—the more spring seems to come and then dances away again—the better the sugaring. You can't do it at all without freezing nights and warm days, which is why the attempt to set up a maple industry in England in the eighteenth century failed: an English spring is too gentle. But it goes further than that. A late wet April snow is simply frustrating for a motorist, or a suburbanite impatient to get to work on his lawn. For a syrup maker it is a cause for rejoicing, because maples run their fastest on such a day. Most of the season you do well to get three or four inches of sap in the bottom of each bucket over a twenty-four-hour period, but on the day of a sugar snow your best buckets fill to the brim and run over. That night you boil until midnight, and there is a holiday atmosphere.

Human beings are not the only creatures who love sugar season. As soon as the first bugs of the year hatch out, they fly unerringly to the nearest sap bucket and gorge. A moth can't drink much, though, and I don't begrudge him his drop or two. I don't even mind the occasional field mouse who makes his way into the sugarhouse and, holding on to the top of the pan with his hind feet, leans way down and drinks half a teaspoonful of partly boiled syrup. But some springs I have had a more formidable rival. Once it was a small brown horse named Dr. Pepper. Dr. Pepper, who belonged to my two daughters, wintered in the front pasture across the road. At the upper end of this pasture is a nice thirty-bucket grove of maples on which I happened to hang my first thirty buckets. For the first several days I got no sap at all, and I thought I must simply have forgotten that they were late trees. Then about the fourth day I noticed half a dozen horsehairs in the first bucket I checked —and then spotted what I should have earlier: that Dr. Pepper had a well-defined path going to every bucket.

I changed all the lids from the hinged kind, which he could (and did) tip up, to the flanged kind that you have to slide off. He instantly learned to slide lids with his teeth. In the end I had to put him in with the beef cattle (I was reluctant to, because he bullies them and takes their hay), but not before losing a hundred gallons or so of sap. Wood-chucks, happily, are too short to reach the buckets.

When sugar season ends, spring has arrived. The maples are budding, which is what makes it end in the first place; the skunk cabbage is out; and fields are completely green. There is still a little mound of snow on the north side of the barn, and there are rims of ice on shady coves in the river. But the incredible luxuriance of our late spring has already begun. Everything but the granite has put out shoots, and even that is likely to have patches of bright green moss.

I am speaking, naturally, of most years. Weather being weather, there is an occasional April when everything stays locked in right through the month. I have not myself lived through such an April, but I have heard about several, and I have read Hosea Beckley's *History of Vermont*, published in 1846. He has much to say about the winter of 1842. That year in April they were three months back in the middle of January. In his own words: "The snow was four feet deep in Brattleboro, the first week in April; and in the

mountain towns, from five to seven. The sleighing contin-
ued about six months."

MAY

*May 19th, 1838. At home all day. Fine weather. Three
hands clearing on hill. Ploughing on meaddowes. James
Beatie was here. He says he has been to Washington [Vt.].
He passed Cabbot mountain. He said the snow was 3
inches deep. . . . Planted the potatoes and sowed the garden seeds. May 22d. At home. Fine weather. All well.
The Canada plum trees are blown out.*

The diary of Henry Stevens of Barnet, Vt.

SPRING LASTS EXACTLY ONE MONTH HERE. The
whole season gets crammed into May. It's hard to say
which is busier, plants or people. May is the month for
setting out trees, spreading manure, planting gardens, fixing fence, buying livestock, cleaning up farms. (By June
the long grass will hide just about any object smaller than
a tractor.) It is also the month when everything that knows
how to blossom does blossom, and everything else grows a
foot longer. As there are occasional sharp frosts throughout
the month, and not only on Cabot Mountain, men and
plants both have to be gamblers.

One sight, one smell, and one sound dominate the first
half of May. The sight is the lovely fresh green of new
grass and new leaves, punctuated at intervals by the blossoms of the serviceberry, by far the earliest tree to flower.
It will have edible berries in June. I am told the Indians
used to use them for making pemmican; on my farm the

birds harvest them so fast I have hardly ever seen a ripe one.

The smell, overwhelming to city nostrils because so organic, is that of the winter manure pile, now dispersed over the fields. I once had a class of college students out about the tenth of May, on a particularly warm, still, high-humidity evening. One boy from Philadelphia kept snuffing the rich air with a worried expression. Finally he said, "Sir, we're not going to get some kind of terrible disease, are we?" I assured him his worst danger was that he might put out leaves.

As for the sound, it's running water. The last snow is going, or has just gone, in the woods. There is still plenty on the mountains. Every stream is running high and cold, and roaring when it comes to a fall or rapids. That's frequently. Especially in the villages, because most settlements were made where there was water power to run a mill or two. Right below the covered bridge in Thetford Center, for example, the Pompy drops fifty feet in a series of rapids and small falls. There are the ruins of five old mills on the banks, and right next to the bridge there is a comparatively new dam. A farmer named Charles Vaughan built it in 1916 and introduced electricity to Thetford. (The lights went off at eleven every night, because Mr. Vaughan shut down his turbine and went to bed.)

When the Army engineers took control of the lower Pompy in 1948, as part of their flood-control program for Hartford, Connecticut, Mr. Vaughan broke a notch in the middle of his dam before shutting the turbine down for good; and until about five years ago the whole river ran through that notch. Most of the year it ran a third or halfway up. In April it filled the notch to the top. But in May it simply obliterated the notch, and ran sheetlike over the whole dam.

Around 1978, the river took a big piece of the dam out, so we no longer have this handy flow-gauge. No matter. At the beginning of May there is so much water that even with half the dam missing it still pours sheetlike across the top, and its solemn roar is audible throughout the village. It is not as impressive as the Stevens River in Barnet, which comes down a cliff and under the main highway, sending (in May) a cloud of mist over half the village and a roar over half the valley, but it will do.

Along about the middle of May, spring visibly shifts gear. It goes into high. For plants this means something new coming into flower or leaf almost every day. For men it means mowing the lawn three times a week, and a rush to get everything transplanted you're going to transplant.

Some of the changes occurring now are comparatively gradual, like the first apple trees coming into blossom a branch at a time, or the lilacs working up for two weeks from bud to flower. Some happen overnight, or seem to. One day there is not a dandelion in sight; the next there is a river of them flowing down the swale in one's pasture. They look so bounteous and so clear a yellow that I have overcome my childhood suburban prejudice and am now almost as fond of dandelions as sheep are. (My daughter Amy's one-time wether, Francis, went through the May of his lambhood eating as many as five hundred or a thousand dandelions daily. He survived to become a notably large sheep.) One day there is nothing to wild strawberries except a few pleasant memories from last year; the next, there are blossoms wherever the meadow grass is poor and thin enough to give them any sun. That means several million blossoms on almost every farm.

Late May is when the gambling occurs. Frost-hating trees are unable to resist the sun any longer, and put out their leaves. The oaks, for example, do. Every few years a really hard frost comes to punish them. Once there was such a frost on a May twenty-second, which I had forgotten about when I noticed on the twenty-eighth that every leaf on every oak on the place had turned black. The maples, the birches, the mountain ash, and every other tree looked fine: I concluded that some new blight must have struck. I cautiously asked a neighbor how his oaks were doing. He looked surprised. "That frost got them, if that's what you mean," he said. A week later each oak had tiny new leaves. They keep a spare set of buds.

Frost-fearing men are able to resist planting their gardens until Memorial Day, but the rest of us are overwhelmed by a desire to beat the weeds. Peas and lettuce don't matter; they laugh at frost. Corn and tomatoes are more delicate. Since corn takes about ten days to come up, men guess when the last frost is likely to be (it usually comes at full moon), and plant nine days earlier. As for tomatoes, one of the commonest sights in the state is everyone rushing out to the tomato bed on a cold evening with blankets and bushel baskets and sap buckets. But we also keep a spare set of seeds.

That's the wrong note to end on, however. May is not a cautious or a suffering month; it's expansive and triumphant. For me its symbol is a certain crab apple tree in the old school district of Rice's Mills, two miles from Thetford Center. (Legally, Rice's Mills is an undifferentiated part of the town of Thetford. The name no longer applies to a school and never was a postal address—it's just a memory. But we all use it.)

This is a particularly large and vigorous crab apple, standing near the base of a southern slope. Its crown of pink blossoms must be thirty feet across. At noon on a sunny day it is a temple of the bees. Portly bumblebees, wasps, hornets, honeybees form a joyful cloud around it and in it. You can hear the many-noted hum before you are near enough to see the largest bee. I think of that scene —the pink sunlit tree, the moving cloud of bees, the hum like a dynamo—as being the closest I'll ever get to Mother Nature personified. That hum and the roar of the Pompy are the two voices of spring. The Pompy's is pure power. The tree's is pure fecundity.

JUNE

Now I return to the Spot where I used to toil and tup at the hoe, & when I meet them [old friends] I feel as though it would be the happy-fying of my days to return and live with them, but the idea of working for a living would dispell all idear of living in Vermont.

The journal of James Guild,
late of Tunbridge, Vt., 1824.

GUILD WAS RIGHT ON BOTH COUNTS. It is the happyfying of one's days to be in Vermont in June—and if one is a farmer, it is too much work. June is hay time. The average farmer has between fifty and a hundred tons to mow, rake, bale—or in rare cases gather loose—and get to the barn.

I have tried it both ways. I have hayed with one neighbor who has a pair of workhorses, a horse-drawn hayloader, a big old blue-painted hay wagon, and a plentiful supply of pitchforks. I have done it with another who has a tractor so big that he can pull a baler and a wagon simultaneously. The baler automatically flips the bales into the wagon. Still, one must stack them as they come, and they come fast. It is almost as hard and hot work as building a load with a pitchfork, though less interesting.

A farmer's whole year is too much work. Milking twice a day (three-quarters of all New England farmers are dairy farmers) 365 days a year, holidays and one's birthday not excepted, is hard work. So is dealing with all that manure. A farmer is endlessly repairing machinery, reroofing barns, fixing fence, laying pipeline, doctoring cattle. Nearly everything that most people call someone else in to do he does for himself, or he couldn't afford to stay in business. It's toil and tup. Which is one reason there were thirty-six thousand farms in Vermont in Guild's time, and the official count now is about fifty-nine hundred. A lot of farmers have decided to cut their workweek down from a hundred hours to forty, and they have taken cushy jobs as loggers, or driving trailer trucks, or maybe they have left Vermont and work in a factory in Connecticut.

At the same time, because you *do* do forty or fifty kinds of work in a month, farming is the most continuously interesting occupation I know. Old-fashioned farming, that is. Being in an enclosed, air-conditioned super-tractor with stereo, plowing a flat, thousand-acre wheat farm in Manitoba must not be all that different from driving a trailer

truck. But behind the horses in Norwich, or on the open tractor in Thetford, mowing up hill and down, one sees the Indian paintbrush come out in early June, and the black-eyed Susans in the middle. One stops to clear the cutter bar and picks a handful of wild strawberries. A rainy day comes, and one shifts to cutting fence posts, or maybe packaging the last of the syrup.

The solution, of course, is to be a serious but part-time farmer. Many people have found it. Those thirty thousand farms that have vanished since Guild's time have by no means all gone back to woods, or turned into summer places, or been developed by sharp-eyed men in Boston. Most of them are farms still. Some are now parts of larger farms. The majority are still independent farms, but part-time, and hence not counted by the Department of Agriculture (even under its new 1975 rules).

A man quits milking, sells his herd and his bulk tank, gets a job in town. But he keeps a few head of beef, and he keeps sugaring. Or a young woman moves to the country, supports herself with a teaching job or a craft, and then buys an old farm to occupy her weekends. Two years later she has learned how to lay stone wall and use a chainsaw, and she has just gotten her first check for the sale of fleeces from her ten sheep. It's a pitifully small check, to be sure.

Farming is a poor way to make a living, at least around here, because you have to go into factory farming to make it pay. It is the best hobby there is—only "hobby" is too little a word. The best way of life. Not just because you learn forty different trades, and not just because you follow the seasons, but because you get to spend your whole life producing a single work of art. That is, the farm itself. You thin a hedgerow here, improve a woodlot there, make a pond across the road. You prune up the old apple trees, and simultaneously make your orchard more beautiful and begin to get good apples again. You keep the beef cattle partly to get the beef, but partly because the pasture looks better when it's grazed. (Envy of how it looks was what led to suburban lawns in the first place.)

Some people make their own bodies a lifetime work of art. It's too small a surface to be worthy of that much attention; and, anyway, for the last thirty or even forty years of the owner's life it's a work of art whose aesthetics steadily diminish. Depressing. Some make their houses and apartments lifetime or longtime works of art. The house at least endures. But again there is not enough scope. When it's all furnished and remodeled and ornamented, there is not much left but dusting and polishing the windows. A farm, on the other hand, can keep on changing and getting more beautiful for a thousand years. A farm is, in fact, an immortal work of art. Maples that I don't even know who planted, back in 1800, line my hay lane. They make a leafy tunnel from which one emerges into the sunlit field. The ones I myself plant I will not live to see as grown trees. But a century from now, if developers don't get hold of the place (and I think I've got things fixed so they can't), they will have become one of the best parts of the view from the kitchen windows. Not to mention a fine addition to the sugar potential.

A part-time farmer who can quit early on a June afternoon to go swimming with his children, who can afford to judge aesthetics equally with profit (as somehow the men who farmed here a hundred and fifty years ago also seemed to), he is happyfied indeed. And when he spends a long June day mowing fields, he is not only getting hay for the winter, he is in effect giving the face of his farm its annual shave, and he is drunk with delight at how well it looks.

JULY

The cupidity of a few land-jobbers . . . gave rise to Vermont as a separate, independent jurisdiction.

The Rev. Hosea Beckley,
History of Vermont, 1846.

To specify each locality in Vermont possessing attractions to the summer tourist, or inducements to one wishing to build a summer home, would require nearly a complete description of each town.

"Resources and Attractions of Vermont,
with a List of Desirable Homes for Sale."
State Board of Agriculture, 1892.

There are said to be 250,000 [milk] cows in the state, which under normal conditions bring in an income of about $22 million a year. Now if 250,000 summer guests could be accommodated . . . it would bring an income into the state of $25 million.

Rural Vermont: A Program for the Future.
By Two Hundred Vermonters, 1931.

JULY IS HERALDED BY TIGER LILIES, by the ripening of wild raspberries (the middle link in the summer-long chain of wild strawberries, raspberries, and blackberries), and by the arrival of the summer people. June was summer (and summer people), too, with plenty of days in the seventies and eighties, and many city dwellers to enjoy them.

July is high summer. It is a relatively quiet time for the landscape—the exuberance of spring is long gone. Pines and spruces, which in late May were growing three inches taller a week, now merely deepen their color. Grass can be mowed once a week. Roaring Branch in Arlington whispers over its rocks; the Mad River in Waitsfield and the Wild Ammonoosuc over in New Hampshire are tamed. My daughters swim where two months ago the Pompy shot through a gorge at twenty miles an hour (or what seemed like it, anyway). Vermont is a settled and permanent green. It is almost impossible to believe that winter ever existed, much less that it will come again.

Only one thing grows wildly in July, and that's the population. All over the state, motels and campgrounds do a peak business. Summer houses are all open. Despite the heat, and July is the one month with a lot of unpleasantly hot weather, carpenters are working busily building new ones. Few of them resemble the white clapboard and brick and stone houses that were already here. Black-toppers are paving driveways into what six months ago were upland pastures and orchards. The highways are crowded (by local standards) with moving vans, U-Haul trucks, and shiny new mobile homes.

For about a hundred years the natives sought this growth. They cultivated out-of-staters as they would any other crop. The visitors, for their part, were content to ripen quietly in their assigned fields—that is, the summer hotels in places like Manchester and Woodstock, the special summer-people villages like Thetford Hill. Or sometimes they would board with a farm family. In any of these ways they contributed nicely to the revenue but didn't much interfere with the landscape.

This has now changed, with, on the whole, dire consequences. Now the visitors want the land. It's worse than a rebellion of the cows would be.

Before the interstate highways came, land in rural Vermont had a value directly based on its productivity. Good farmland might cost you as much as two hundred dollars per acre; rocky hillside went for ten dollars. Summer-people land, of course, went for a lot more, but that was mostly limited to a narrow strip around each lake and around certain villages. Elsewhere, you could buy a hundred acres knowing that if you chose to work it, the land would yield enough to pay the taxes and a modest return besides. If you didn't, you restored forest and deer.

Now the value of land is based on its potential for development. If your field could be a subdivision with not too much expense for putting the roads through, it is suddenly worth a thousand—or two thousand or three thousand— an acre, and you are taxed on that basis. Even though as working land it earns no more than it did ten years ago. Even though all you want to do is keep Holsteins on it or raise cucumbers. A Vermont farm has come to be like a speculative stock, which pays an annual dividend of twenty cents a share but is priced at eighty-five dollars. With this difference: that the stock speculator pays no tax until and if he sells, but the farmer may face an annual tax bill larger than the whole income from his farm. Only the very rich (which as many as two Vermont farmers are) can afford the taxes on much development land. And there is now no other kind.

The state is perfectly aware of this problem and has passed a law providing that anyone in the state may deed his or her development rights to any one of several state agencies, such as the Fish and Game Department. (It, of course, would not exercise them—couldn't; it doesn't own the land.) Since most of the cash value of a Vermont farm lies in the possibility of cutting it up into building lots, the assessment would promptly plummet, and the farmer could once again afford his taxes. The only problem is that as the state has not yet appropriated a penny to implement the bill, the state agencies adamantly refuse to be given any development rights.

Fortunately, there is a very active private group called the Ottauquechee Regional Land Trust which has started collecting some, and there are one or two smart towns such as Pomfret that will accept them. And the state *has* recently put some money behind a moderately useful land-use tax law.

Meanwhile, the transfer of land moves steadily forward from native farmers to out-of-state land jobbers and a few in-state ones. And from them in small but costly parcels to people who want to summer in Colonial Village, formerly the Perkins place. One of the commonest July sights is the auction notice at the village store, beginning "As I have discontinued farming . . ."

It's perfectly true that in this, as in all forty-nine other states, there is a long history of land exploitation, and that the best people were often most active in it. Who do Vermonters look back on as the chief of the founding fathers? Ethan and Ira Allen. The Allen brothers were both dedicated land speculators, and they were not the first. But eighteenth-century speculation was different. For example, when an ambitious speculator like Thomas Brantingham of New York City bought sixteen thousand acres of Vermont land in 1792, he in no way inconvenienced the trout or the bears, much less brought in a series of burger stands. Even if Brantingham had succeeded in developing the land, it would simply have become about a hundred Vermont farms—fewer bears, in that case, but more cows.

The corporate developers now are less beneficial. The sale of sixteen thousand acres is likely to mean twelve thousand ski chalets, two golf courses, a bowling alley, another denuded mountain, a shopping mall, and a further small decline in cows and maple syrup.

All is not lost. Part-time farmers, when they can afford it, are buying a good deal of the land. An occasional man who can't bear to see a two-hundred-year-old work of art bulldozed deeds his farm entire to the town or the state. The legislature continues slowly to improve the laws. And nature is not quite idle, either. Even as developers move into Vermont from the southeast, coyotes are moving in from the northwest. We may strike a new balance yet.

AUGUST

We have no populous towns, seaports, or large manufactories, to collect the people together. They are spread over the whole country, forming small and separate settlements.

Samuel Williams, 1794.

I DON'T EVEN KNOW HOW MANY separate settlements there are in Vermont. There are two hundred thirty-seven *towns*, plus our nine cities. Subtract the hundred thousand people who live in the nine cities from the half million in the state, and that leaves an average of seventeen hundred people per town. (Nearer three thousand in August.) Reasonably small, yes.

But a New England town is like a midwestern township. It is a unit of government, it generally covers thirty-six square miles, and it has nothing much to do with where people actually live. In the town of Thetford, for example, there are either five and a half or six settlements, depending on who's counting. East Thetford and North Thetford are river villages, two miles apart, on the banks of the Connecticut. I would guess each has a couple of hundred people. (Since a settlement has no legal boundaries, only subjective ones, it has to be a guess.) Each has a post office, a garage, and a store. East Thetford also has a doctor, a dentist, a small furniture factory, and a good country restaurant. North Thetford has a remarkably fine source of used car parts, a stone hotel, and a Congregational church. One of the few in the country, I am told, with a gold pineapple on top of the steeple.

Thetford Hill sits on top of the first high ridge you come to when you start west from the river—five hundred feet above East Thetford. It has a stunning view back into New Hampshire; it has the town high school, alias Thetford Academy; it has about ninety residents in the winter and at least three hundred in the summer. Also the original (1773) and still biggest church in town, and a post office. No stores.

Go down the other side of the ridge, and in a mile you come to Thetford Center, strung out along the Pompy. Once it had an ax factory and a shutter mill. (That's why nearly all the old houses in town have the same highly distinctive shutter pattern.) It still has a post office, a store, one of the best mechanics in the state, the town hall, a beautiful little brick Methodist church, and two hundred people.

Keep going, and in another four miles, just before you reach the western border of the town, there's another rapid on the Pompy, and the village of Post Mills. It was formerly the site of a fishing-rod factory. Currently it's dominated by a mill that makes blanks for chair legs out of rock maple and yellow birch logs, though it also has two rival general stores and a markedly rural airport. I still haven't mentioned Union Village, which is half in the town of Thetford and half in the town of Norwich—hence the name—or Sawney Bean, a sort of semi-community up in the highest valley in town.

In August most of these settlements are busy celebrating their separateness. Thetford Hill has a fair the first week in August, a very elegant and mannered fair. Union Village puts on two church suppers during the month, and North Thetford celebrates with an all-day fete and auction. In the Center we had our fair, called Old Home Day, back in July.

Over the whole state there must be hundreds of such suppers and fetes and fairs. If I had time and appetite, I think I would go to them all. I *have* been to a good many. Ranging from the heartrendingly small, like the sugar-on-snow supper held each April in the basement of the two-room schoolhouse in Vershire, to the large and bustling, like Norwich Fair. That has ox-pulling contests, and a Ferris wheel, and the kind of high-velocity, eccentric-orbit carnival rides that can make a strong man sick for two days, but that teenage girls will go on three times in a row and just look more rosy-cheeked.

One reason for going to suppers and fairs is simply that it gives you a chance to see the villages they're held in. There are almost no beautiful cities in America, though there are many beautiful parts of cities, and some sections that are glorious without being beautiful, like downtown Chicago. Cities are too big and too rich for beauty; they have outgrown themselves too many times. Seen from a distance, so that they seem little again—like New York viewed from the harbor, or almost any city perceived as a jewel-pattern of lights when you fly over it at night—they are indeed beautiful, but that's another matter.

A settlement of a few hundred people, on the other hand, has never outgrown itself. It has no sections; it's all one piece. If most of its houses were built in the late eighteenth and early nineteenth centuries, and if the whole village is set in green hills, it stands an excellent chance of being beautiful. Many villages in Vermont are.

Another reason to go, of course, is the food. Different settlements pride themselves on different specialties. Union Village is very strong on chicken pie. Thetford Center is famous—within a ten-mile radius—for red flannel hash. In Fairlee they import lobsters. Lyme, New Hampshire, is all casseroles.

If you work at the supper, as opposed to just going, or if you have a friend in the kitchen, you can even help support your farm. The first year I ever kept pigs, my little boar and sow lived throughout August and well into September on a stunningly good diet of scrapings—unfinished corn on the cob, homemade piecrust left on plates by people who don't eat the crust even of pie made by the best cook in Sawney Bean, and so on. A good supper will yield you forty pounds.

Even apart from the fairs, August is a good month. The baby carrots, the little Cow Horn potatoes, the first plums are finally ready to eat. It is still high summer and good for swimming, but there are many days when it gets cool enough at night so that you can burn off the paper that's been accumulating in the wood stove. Sometime about the middle of the month, the morning mists begin. Each day when they clear, you get the kind of weather that can only be described as blessed. All colors and shapes are unusually distinct, even the corners of shadows seem extra sharp, and even in hot sun there is the faintest hint of chill. Yet you are not cold.

Best of all is when such a mist comes on in the late evening, instead of at dawn, and one is awake to see it arrive. There is a two-hundred-foot hill across the road. Once my wife, Nan, and I climbed it at midnight in late August. The moon wasn't full, but it was bright—that was what had tempted us out in the first place.

Five minutes after we reached the top, a puff of mist came round the valley wall, heading upriver from Union Village. In half an hour we were on a moonlit island above a valley full of mist. By one o'clock the mist had lapped up over the hilltop, and we had watched our view shorten from seven miles (the hills beyond Post Mills) to a hundred feet. We had seen the nearest tree line fade and become ghostly, and then vanish, and finally we started down in a faintly luminous white cloud. We got very wet.

Such nights are exceptional. Any day in August is good for driving to a village or two, though. Villages are the thing to see, as the American painter Charles Eldridge realized a long time ago. Eldridge, an extremely urbane young man from Hartford, Connecticut, paid a visit to

Vermont in 1833. He was going to Montpelier on the stagecoach. Since he knew Montpelier to be the state capitol, he figured it must be a sort of lesser Hartford. It wasn't. Still isn't. The population has yet to reach ten thousand, and was about thirty-seven hundred then. Not many monumental buildings, either. "We were disappointed in the view," Eldridge wrote, "and felt a little chagrin, that in point of size and elegance, we had expected too much of Montpelier." Then he stopped to consider why. "But in fact there had been in our route, many villages too beautiful to have a superior even in the principal town."

SEPTEMBER

The fact is, the American climate is thoroughly and irredeemably bad—the very worst in the world . . . and I conceive nothing can make up for this dreadful and important defect.

Rambles in the United States and Canada
During the Year 1845.
By "Rubio" [Thomas H. James, an Englishman].

RUBIO HAS SOMETHING THERE. Most of the time, most of this country is either too hot or too cold. In the East, it's rather often too muggy as well.

But there are exceptions. It would have been a pleasure to bring Rubio to Thetford in September and watch him look frantically for something to dislike. Better weather doesn't occur. The occasional mists of August are now a regular thing, with the result that every morning the sun rises with power enough to send the dew steaming up from roofs—and then the valleys fill with light cloud, and the sunlight slowly fades. The morning stays fresh and cool for about four hours. Then the sun burns through again, and a clear day follows, crisp and golden.

All creatures respond to the winy air. If you call your two Hereford cattle for their daily quart of grain, they come at the first shout (in July they didn't even look up until the third), and they come at a rocking bovine canter, out of pure high spirits. Sedentary men are to be seen climbing mountains. Even a house cat will sometimes charge across the lawn and let his momentum take him ten feet up a maple, just to show how good he feels. It is ideal harvest weather. There is finally plenty of corn. If it weren't for the frost that's looming ahead now, certain to kill the garden, and if it weren't for the yellow leaves that begin to appear as warnings on birches and elms, Vermonters might forget in September that they are not supposed to be optimists.

Not only the weather is smiling. One of the delights of a farm is that a dozen times a year you have a profusion of something—more watermelons or blueberries or walnuts than you can possibly use. You possess an innocent and prodigal wealth. It is the opposite remove from the little pinched economies of supermarket buying—the four "tomatoes" in a cellophane package, the single cantaloupe for ninety-nine cents. (I was going to say the single pumpkin for two-fifty, until I realized most supermarkets don't even *have* pumpkins. They sell objects made of orange plastic.)

Vermont is no cornucopia as farmland goes, but we have our times of profusion, too, and the greatest of them comes in September. Apples. There's hardly a farm in the state that doesn't have apple trees along half the fence lines, and an old apple orchard besides. Even in deep woods you constantly come on old apple trees bearing away—half-forgotten species like Pound Sweets and Greenings.

There is a fine careless freedom in walking through the orchard the first week in September, testing an apple from each tree to see if it's ripe—taking one bite and then tossing it away. No harm in that; it will go back to humus.

Not that it always gets a chance, this early in the season. Deer adore apples, and a few hours later you are likely to see a young doe approach the orchard at a brisk trot. She circles the first tree, she finds and eats your bitten apple and the one windfall that has come down since her last visit. Then she trots to the next tree. If not enough apples are down, sometimes she will stand on her hind legs and begin picking from the lower branches. September is the second-best month for watching deer.

By the middle of the month most apples *are* ripe. (Duchesses were ripe in August, and people were busy making pink applesauce.) Now the scene is like a Breughel painting. Men with their own barrels are gathered at the cider mills, laying in a winter's supply. The smaller commercial orchards, these days run mostly on a pick-your-own basis, swarm with people and pickup trucks and bushel baskets. Every small child has an apple in one hand that he is eating and an apple in the other that he (now) thinks he is going to eat immediately afterward.

Some of the part-time farmers are fortunate enough to have one of the old home cider presses that Sears Roebuck sold by the thousand at the turn of the century, or one of the new ones small companies have been making for the past ten years. Both consist of a hand-turned grinder and a press with a capacity of one bushel, all mounted as one neat unit. A few people are still more fortunate and also have an old nineteenth-century chopper—one or two part-time blacksmiths in Vermont have started making them again—and its accompanying giant wooden bowl.

On a particularly golden Sunday afternoon a few Septembers ago, I was one of a dozen people gathered at such a farm. Most of us had glass or plastic cider jugs we had brought with us. On this particular place it is the wife who does most of the part-time farming, and she had a light wagon hitched to her driving mare, Chiquita, so that we could all move through the orchard tossing apples in together. In half an hour we gathered a dozen bushels, not worrying in the least about bruises or rust, because these apples were about to become cider. Not worrying about pesticides, either, because this orchard is unsprayed.

Then for a couple of hours we took turns chopping apples in the great wooden bowl, running them through the grinder (one to turn the handle and one to keep feeding chunks of apple in), and pressing them. We wound up with ten gallons of cider, a lot of unused apples, and about a hundred pounds of pomace, which is what is left after you grind apples and press them.

Pomace is to horses as chocolate bars are to teenagers, and most of this went to our hostess's work team. But one basketful I brought home to my pigs. Pigs love pomace so much that they got into an ugly fight—easily settled, however, by my shaking down and throwing them a couple of hundred apples from a tree near their pen. Then I walked over to the garden to get some fresh corn for supper. We had almost had a frost the night before—the temperature had dropped to thirty-three—but the mist had arrived just in time to save us, and the corn was unhurt. On the way back I tossed the stalks to the pigs—pigs dote on cornstalks —and I noticed that one maple over on Houghton Hill had overnight turned bright red.

OCTOBER

All the hills blush; I think autumn must be the best season to journey over even the Green Mountains. You frequently exclaim to yourself, what red maples!

Henry David Thoreau, 1850.

A solitary maple on a woodside flames in single scarlet, recalls nothing so much as the daughter of a noble house dressed for a fancy ball, with the whole family gathered round to admire her before she goes.

Henry James,
The American Scene, 1907.

OCTOBER BELONGS TO THE TREES. There is already a good deal of color when the month begins, especially along the roads. In fact, there is considerably more than there was in Thoreau's time or Henry James's. This is not because of any change in the climate, but because of a change in the way we take care of the roads.

Back when they came tree-looking—I won't use the insulting term "leaf-peeping"—every road in the state was dirt. Salt was something you used in making salt pork. Winter road care consisted of packing the snow down with giant rollers, to assure a good sleighing surface.

About fifty years ago rolling went out and plowing came

44

in. It didn't hurt the trees a bit, except occasionally when the plow nicked one. For that matter, it didn't even keep the roads from staying snowy most of the winter. The layer of snow on top of the dirt was just much thinner (and mud season somewhat shorter). Present-day dirt roads still are white in the winter, which is why they get photographed so much.

The trouble came with paving. That is, quite recently. Twenty years ago not only most back roads but some state highways and even a couple of far-northern stretches of U.S. 5 were dirt. Now most are paved. A paved road can't have a layer of snow, or else some of it melts and refreezes as ice, and everybody skids and has accidents. On with the salt. Handy for cars, maybe necessary for large trucks, but terrible for trees. Their roots pick up the salt in the spring, and they slowly sicken and die.

Meanwhile, they put on a splendid show. A sick tree turns color and sheds a trifle earlier each year, so that most roadside trees are now two weeks to a month ahead of the rest. On October first sugar maples by the road are orange —or already bare—elms are yellow, birches are speckled with lemon color. A brave sight, even though it's the flush of disease.

Away from the roads the landscape is still green. You do see bits of scarlet here and there, which are the sumacs and the red maples. A red maple in the fall is about the reddest thing there is. A strong bold peasant red—noble trees don't rush off to the ball quite so early. You also see some intense yellow where an ash has pulled its usual trick of turning every leaf exactly the same color at exactly the same instant. Bright red and bright yellow. Since the blue skies of September persist and even get bluer in October, hills and

45

sky make a simple pattern of primary colors, with a green background.

As the month progresses, complexity sets in. Trees whose names I don't even know turn a dozen shades of carmine and vermilion and ocher and jonquil. Ferns go bronze; the briers become a deep, lustrous maroon. By the time the fall foliage tours peak in mid-month, every hillside has fifty or so hues to offer. The sugar maple, lord of our trees at any time, rules especially now. A single sugar maple is capable of producing two or three shades of orange, pink, and yellow on just one branch; a grove of them offers such richness of color that the eye can hardly take it in. A four-year-old girl once gave sugar maples their ultimate praise. She and her mother were collecting leaves in a particularly glowing grove, and when she had picked about a bushel, all different, she looked up and said thoughtfully, "Mummy, God must spend an awful lot of money on fall."

By late October the fancy-dress ball is over. Oaks in their sensible brown remain, and beeches in gossamer tan, and the evergreens. But all other trees are bare except a few yellow poplars, now going fast. The grass is almost done growing, and in a heavily grazed pasture you are beginning to feed hay. The first killing frost has come. Just exactly when varies not only from year to year but from farm to farm. On mine, which is near but not quite at the bottom of the valley through which the Pompy runs, it has come as late as October sixteenth and as early as August thirty-first. But come it has, and the garden is dead. There is nothing left to harvest but a little late lettuce and the last cider apples. The land is through working for the year.

Men, on the other hand, still have plenty to do. A part-time farmer, indeed, is almost as busy as he was in May, because October is the last month there will be any daylight left when he gets home from work. October days are perhaps the best of the whole year, fresher and cleaner even than those of September, but they are too short. You feel pushed. Provident men are out in the short afternoons cutting next year's wood supply; improvident men are rustling up this year's wood, which they will have to burn green. If you want early peas next spring, you had better prepare the ground now, before it freezes. There are all those storm windows to put up. If you neglected to wash your sap buckets in April, you frantically do it in October. And meanwhile the crisp golden weather tempts you not to work at all. A Saturday when you could perfectly well cut half a cord of red maple in the morning, and wash ten storm windows after lunch, and rake a truckload of leaves before dark, you walk up Potato Hill with a sandwich, getting all the views you never got while the leaves were on, picking a few butternuts the squirrels missed, maybe seeing a fox.

Then one morning at the very end of the month, you go out to feed the pigs, and it's twenty above, and the water in their trough is frozen solid, and you know you must make a last steady drive to get ready before winter comes.

NOVEMBER

There the seasons stopped awhile. Autumn was gone, Winter was not. We had Time dealt out to us—more, clear, fresh Time—grace-days to enjoy.

Rudyard Kipling,
"Seasons in Brattleboro," 1895.

47

THOSE GRACE-DAYS DON'T come every year. About one year in two, November starts with rain, moves on to sleet, and by the middle settles in to snow. The first year I ever kept cows, for example, I wasn't dealt one extra minute to finish building their winter shelter. The first week of November was mostly rain. The second mostly snow (which often melted again, to be sure). There was a minor blizzard on the thirteenth—bad enough to knock a few trees down across U.S. 5. Then a little more snow on the sixteenth. More still on the seventeenth, and that day my seven-year-old daughter had the first snowmobile ride of her life. (She had been skiing since she was five, though she admittedly started early. They don't teach it in the schools here until second grade.)

But the other half of the years, November is a whole grace-month, until locking begins at the very end. Clear skies, pleasant days (pitifully short), and lots of free time. There is always *some* work on a farm, of course. November is when pigs get butchered, and lambs, too. There is hay to feed out; there are stoves to keep burning.

Mostly, though, November time is one's own. The trees are bare: no more leaves to rake. The house is banked, the woodshed full, and you have a fresh-cut eight or ten cords stacked out in the woods. A mild sunny weekend is a time either go to hunting or exploring. Or, if you don't have a red shirt and a red hat, a time to stay strictly indoors. Deer season has begun.

My own choice is to go exploring. Like the rest of rural New England, Vermont is full of ruins where there were once farms. And not only farms, but copper mines and gristmills and little mountain graveyards. Some of these last are still dimly in use. There is one about three miles from my farm that had frequent burials from 1770 to 1900 and has had about one a generation since. It also has one of the prettiest views in the region. Sometime early in the twenty-first century I mean to move down there. I realize I won't get much good from the view, but I still want to be where it is.

There are two ways to go exploring in this kind of country. One is simply to start out in a more or less straight line and see what you come to. You usually just come to woods and more woods, occasionally crossing a dirt road or skirting a still-active farm. The chief pleasure is that now with all the leaves down you can see every old stone wall, where there were once fields and pastures, and you can marvel yet again at the beauty of all that forgotten stonework, and the skill of the makers. You can also see here and there a three-hundred-year-old oak or maple the settlers spared.

But now and again you find something more. My best November find was up near Five Corners, which sounds heavily settled but isn't. My wife and I were walking up one of the five roads that make the corners—one no longer passable for cars—and came on a fallen-in house. Usually there's not much to see except a lot of rotten clapboards and fallen timbers, and not much to do except fall through the floor yourself and break a leg. This had been a glorious house in its time, though, and even in its decay you could walk cautiously around part of the first floor. Doing so, you came into the living room, and found that it had been plastered so well a hundred and fifty years ago that on two walls the plaster was still sound. And on the plaster some long-ago farmer's wife had painted designs. There were patterns of leaves, and sunbursts, and on either side of the fireplace little groups of prancing horses, three inches high.

It seems to me that in museums I see bits of homely Roman mosaic and not very interesting painted Greek vases—neither half so nice to look at as those prancing horses. In the spring we went back with a friend who is an art historian, but the rest of the house had fallen down. We had five feet of snow that winter.

The other way to explore, of course, is with a definite goal in mind. Mine has usually been to find bricks. My farmhouse, when I bought it, had a dirt floor in the cellar, as old farmhouses generally do. Little by little I have paved the cellar with eighteenth- and nineteenth-century bricks, most of them found in the woods. Seventeen cellar holes and the smelter from one old copper mine are represented.

The charm of old bricks, apart from their being free, lies in their extreme individuality (as bricks go). A good many have finger- and thumbprints on one side, from where they were picked up and put in the kiln to be fired. Most vary slightly in size. Twice I have found bricks that were dated with the tip of someone's finger. But mostly the brick hunt is an excuse to prowl through the woods with an old town map, locating cellar holes. Once you've found one, you play amateur archaeologist, guessing what sort of house it was, where the barn stood, trying to locate the spring. An armload of rosy old bricks is just a bonus.

The last week of November such games come to an abrupt end. Winter doesn't necessarily begin, but locking does. Sometime within a week on either side of Thanksgiving the ground freezes, not to thaw again until spring. Henceforth any rummaging in cellar holes would have to be done with a pickax. Few animals are to be seen in the woods now. The deer are hiding from the hunters, and most small animals are underground or inside trees until spring. I am ready to be indoors myself.

D E C E M B E R

I have cause to remember [Royalton, Vermont] for its wilderness aspect, it abounds with Pine, a thin flashy kind of soil; but what few people inhabit it appear to live tolerable.

John Russell Davis,
*Diary of a Journey Through
Massachusetts, Vermont, and Eastern New York,* 1800.

DAVIS WROTE THAT IN JUNE. In December he might have been less sure. December is the bleakest month of the year. No more grace-days now. Just cold and darkness, both steadily increasing.

These are drawbacks Vermont shares with most of the Northern Hemisphere, of course, but both conditions seem especially pronounced here. We are at a higher latitude than people sometimes realize. A man I know left the state a few years ago and moved south. Where he went was Canada. The city of London, Ontario, to be precise, which is a hundred and twenty-five miles south of where he started. If he'd gone to Kingsville, he would have been two hundred miles south, blinking in the sun.

The darkness at least increases in a known and predictable way—and furthermore, by the end of the month the days will have reached their shortest and be growing longer again. The cold is trickier. December begins almost gently.

Some years there is snow, and some years there's not. Every year there is gradual locking: little ponds skin over and then big ones. No lakes yet. Every year dreary cold days alternate with almost as dreary mild ones. There is an overwhelming sense of waiting for something to happen.

Then it happens. With sudden savage force, winter begins. The date may be as early as December fifth, or as late as the twentieth.

One night you wake up cold and pull up another blanket. No use—you're still cold. In the morning you look at the thermometer and it has dropped to eight below. Yesterday the Pompy and the Connecticut were open water. Today they are ice, except for one smoking patch just below the Ledyard Bridge on the Connecticut, and a few rapids on the Pompy that send gusts of steam fifty feet into the air. A few laboring furnaces break down that night. Several careless newcomers to the state have their first experience with frozen water pipes the next morning. Many cars won't start. From now until spring, life is going to be stern.

When you add that by Christmas there is certain to be somewhere between a foot and two feet of snow on the ground, and probably a terrific ice storm, there seems a certain madness in staying here at all. And yet we not only live tolerable, in some ways we live well. That will remain true as long as the state has its wilderness aspect.

A frozen forest with rivers and lakes in it is a wonderfully accessible place, almost a magical one. There is no magic to a city or a suburban street in cold weather, and not much shelter, either. People simply get to where they're going, the fastest way possible. But a winter forest is a place to go for pleasure.

It's true you had better dress warmly if you plan to be

out long; it's also true that the forest itself will shield you. The wind may whistle down city streets, but in woods with any quantity of evergreens (and this state still abounds with Pine, not to mention Hemlock, Spruce, and Cedar), there are innumerable calm glades. In December you can reach them all. The swamps you stayed out of in November you now casually stroll through; a pond is no barrier, but a shortcut. There are places you can skate ten miles up a river on the new ice and never meet a soul.

Even nicer is going out on foot with one's children to find a Christmas tree. Bringing a tree home is a pleasure even if you only drive to a shopping center and pay nine dollars for one commercially grown. To prowl through your own woods, considering a tall young pine here and a trim little hemlock there, is delight. Finally you spot a six-foot spruce with especially shapely branches, you let one of the children cut it, and you drag it home in triumph.

Even when heavy snow comes, the woods are a place to go. Now you set out on skis or by snowmobile; and though the days are short, the sun is bright and the ground so dazzling that it hardly seems men have soiled this planet at all. (An illusion, of course. If we have acid rain all summer, we must get acid snow all winter. But the flakes still look pure enough.)

For some reason it seems nearly always to snow on the last day of the year. Sixteen of the twenty-one December thirty-firsts that I have records for, there has been at least a flurry. The best years, enough falls to cover all things freshly, but not enough to make driving difficult.

One such New Year's Eve I was at a party in a farmhouse on a hill above a small Vermont village. By midnight the snow had stopped and the moon had come out. It was one

53

degree below zero. Almost everyone at the party threw on a coat, shoved on boots, and came outside to look at the new snow. All around was a silence so total that the world seemed not merely cleansed but newly created. Nowhere was there the sound of a car in that hushed world, or so much as a dog barking. The clear moonlight revealed no mess, either. Men live in Vermont; no doubt there were plastic bags and even abandoned refrigerators within easy walking distance. They were nullified by the snow.

To be outdoors on such a night is to experience that awe which modern man is said to have lost the capacity for, but which he has really just ceased to look for in the right places.

Part II

~~

Part I.2

Winter Escape

THE MONTH WAS JANUARY. The time, 7:10 on a Saturday morning; the place, a farm in eastern Vermont; the temperature, three below zero.

A father (me) and two daughters (Elisabeth and Amy) have been up late talking, and are still asleep. The phone rings, and Amy, whose room is nearest the phone, jumps up to answer. It's Mary Mallary up the road. "Tell your dad one of his cows is out," she says.

One minute later Amy is shaking me. I groan and get up. This wouldn't happen if I had dairy cattle. They'd be in the barn. But our Herefords stay out all winter.

From the front kitchen window I can see their pasture, which is right across the road. The cows—we only have two—are both right where they should be: standing impatiently by the hay feeder, waiting for breakfast. But I see only one calf with them. I sigh, pull on my boots, and go out.

As I do, there's a quick snort from behind the lilac bush. The big bull calf, the one Elisabeth named Armand, comes racing across the lawn. There are only three inches of snow on the ground—a rare thing for us in January—and he is as free to run as if it were summer. The sub-zero air just makes him feel good. He reaches the road, and trots daintily up toward Mallary's.

I get my trusty grain bucket from the barn. I remember gratefully that the two mothers have been letting their calves share the morning snack of grain for the last month. Armand thus knows about grain and grain buckets; with any luck he will follow me (or at least the bucket) right back into the pasture.

Near the hay feeder there is a little gate that leads into the pasture. By the time I get over there and open it, Armand is trotting back down the road to see what I have in the bucket. A car with New York plates also comes down the road. It slows down, and the driver shouts to me, "Hey, Mister, your cow's out." I wave to show I've heard, and hope that he won't linger and make Armand nervous. He doesn't. He drives on, his duty done.

Armand is interested in the bucket, but he won't come up to me. He stands ten feet away, tossing his miniature bull head. Meanwhile, the two mothers and the other calf peer out the open gate, eager to get at the bucket. I shoo them back in, and pour some grain to keep them busy.

A neighbor, a girl in her twenties, drives past, sees what is happening, and stops. She doesn't inform me my calf is out; she comes to help me drive him in. But Armand is too quick for us. He snorts and runs rapidly downhill toward the covered bridge. I tell her I can manage, and she gets back in her car and drives on.

By now I am very cold. Sub-zero weather doesn't exhilarate me a bit. I go in the house and put on some more clothes. Meanwhile Armand comes trotting back up, right in the middle of the road. I emerge. He sees me, and runs under a little clump of hemlocks at the end of our driveway. Some instinct has told him that I can't get under those low branches, and that he is safe there.

I get more grain, and a rope. I walk slowly toward the hemlocks. Armand backs up. I set the bucket down in the middle of the driveway, and casually walk back ten feet. Armand comes cautiously out, keeping one eye on me.

As soon as his nose is in the bucket, I begin to tiptoe forward.

Armand's eye is still on me. He dances back a few feet. I freeze. (Two senses.) The grain is delicious, and after a minute he returns. Four times we repeat this maneuver. By then I am almost to the bucket, and his nose is back in. Quick as a wink I put the rope around his bull neck. Quicker than half a wink, he leaps straight in the air, pulls free, and dashes back under the hemlocks. Round Two to Armand.

I am now out of ideas. I've already spent the best part of an hour on Armand. And what I'm dying for (besides seeing him back behind barbed wire) is a cup of hot coffee. I go inside and make one. I also call Floyd Dexter—the man who sold me Armand's mother, the man from whom I've learned more about farming than from any other three people put together. Floyd is in his sixties, and has known pretty much all about cattle for fifty years. Part of me wanted to call him when I first got up. But if you keep cattle, you ought to be able to catch them when they get out.

What I actually *ask* Floyd for is advice on what to do next. But my heart leaps up when he says he'll be over to help in fifteen minutes. I finish my coffee, get my fencing tools, and go across the road to find the place where Armand got out. Armand himself remains under the hemlocks.

I find the place easily. Ten years ago, when I was a lot more ignorant than I am now, I bought some Belgian wire from Sears and Roebuck. According to the friendly Sears catalogue, it was a lot lighter than regular barbed wire, and just as strong. This is true. But it is also a lot more brittle —and when a piece breaks, it coils up like a spring, mangling anything in its path as it comes. It breaks quite readily at three below, a kind of weather they don't have any of in Belgium. For the past nine years I have been buying soft, heavy American or Canadian wire. I get scratched roughly one-tenth as much.

There is still some of the light Belgian wire on the road side of the pasture, and in one place the bottom strand has broken. I have just finished patching the break with new wire when Floyd arrives.

Floyd looks at Armand under the hemlocks, and at the other three cattle who are now eating a bale of hay I brought them earlier. He then teaches me roughly the thirty-ninth lesson he has taught me about cattle-keeping.

"That little fellow's going to want some hay," he says. "If you go away, he'll start eating. But he'll do it from this side of the fence. What you want to do is get them others feeding well inside the pasture, so's he'll *have* to go in."

Too late, I tell him. I've already got a bale in the feeder, and they'll be working on that all morning.

"Oh, no," he says, giving me my fortieth lesson. "You put in some fresh hay, cattle'll always leave what they're eating, and go try it." So I get another bale, and we scatter it on the snow fifty feet inside the little gate. The two mothers instantly head for it, followed after a minute by the other calf.

Armand, who is watching, doesn't like it when his mother vanishes from the fence. Soon he is back across the road, being careful to keep his distance from Floyd, me, and the open gate. We stand perfectly still. Armand is visibly thinking. He goes up to within six feet of the gate, sees his mother inside, sees the new hay, starts to go in. Then he hesitates. We are cold, and sick of the whole business. We decide to encourage him by slowly closing in from both sides, our arms out like scarecrows.

Armand snorts and tries to dash back to the hemlocks. We head him off. For a while we have him dancing in a circle, always a little nearer the gate. Then he puts on a burst of speed, and gets past us. Soon he is in Mary Mallary's side yard and heading over to Paige's. Floyd looks disgusted. "All my fault," he says. "If we'd just waited two-three more minutes, he'd a gone in by hisself."

"Floyd, it's really my fault," I answer. "I *had* that rope almost around his neck, more than an hour ago. If I'd just been a little more patient, he'd have been back in long ago."

Floyd smiles. "He might," he says. "But I doubt it. That little fellow's five months old, and stronger'n hang. If you'd got that rope on him, there's no way you could have held him. Either he'd a dragged you right down to the covered bridge, or he'd a broke loose—and then you'd never have kept a rope on him again. Neck rope's no way to lead even a calf." Lesson #41.

Now we trudge up to Mallary's, and gradually head Armand back toward the gate. He is just starting his famous gate dance again, when a pickup truck pulls over. A farmer we both know and his son get out. It's Junior Hodge. Without saying a word, they join our circle. Four is too many for Armand: there is no hole for him to break through. He trots through the gate meek as a lamb—and then charges down to the new hay. A few seconds later he is chewing as placidly as if he'd never been out of a pasture in his life.

By now it is nine-thirty, and I'm not even cold anymore. This is a bright, sunny morning, and the temperature is already up to fifteen above. I'm about as hungry, though, as a man can get.

I've also worked out for myself Rule #42, which Floyd doesn't even have to teach me. (He wouldn't have, anyway. He's too polite.) It reads as follows: The sure way to tell a true countryman is not by his clothes, or the dilapidation of his truck, or even his accent. It's by how he responds to cattle on the road. A true countryman, even if he were on his way to his wedding, would stop and help you drive them back in.

That spirit of instant cooperation, in fact, is what keeps the countrymen ahead of the cows. After all, the cows are stronger.

A One-Horsepower Mower

THERE ARE SEVERAL WAYS to deal with the lawn around a country house. The simplest—and most suburban—is to buy a large power mower, and spend half a day every week mowing it.

A more interesting way is to fence off the part farthest from the house, and then get a couple of lambs. Let them do the mowing. In the fall you have a reduced gasoline bill, plus a hundred pounds of meat for the freezer, and two sheepskins to put on chairs. Several years ago I adopted this method.

I quickly discovered, though, that I had a problem. Lawns and lambs are not well timed. In the spring, when grass grows fastest, lambs are still too young to eat much. They can't even keep up with a pasture made out of one side of a yard. In the fall, when they are big and greedy, the grass quits growing.

Real farmers do not encounter this problem. Real farmers have animals of all sizes at all times of year. Grown sheep can and do keep up with spring grass. The ewes even transmit quite a lot of it to the lambs in the concentrated form of milk. But my two annual weanlings can hardly make a dent in a quarter-acre pasture. By the first of June, most of the grass is a foot high. Worse yet, it is already too tough for young lambs, so they keep grazing and regrazing the few open patches. My once-elegant piece of lawn looks as if it had the mange. With a sigh, I set the power mower as high as it will go, and go out to waste gasoline.

This past June I had a better idea. Instead of a three-horsepower mower, I would use a one-horsepower horse. A particularly speedy model happened to be available. Speedy at mowing, that is, not at galloping.

Pioneer friends of mine named George deNagy and Merry Leonard have a Belgian workhorse, which they use in logging, and they are habitually short of pasture for him. So I invited them to bring Chub over for a visit. I knew, from George's frequent complaints about it, that Chub had been eating two bales of hay a day all winter—eighty or ninety pounds of food a day. I figured that with an appetite like that, he could bring the lamb pasture to velvety smoothness in a week or less. I was right, too. I just hadn't foreseen all the side effects.

Merry rode the horse over on Saturday afternoon. She is a tall, good-looking, strongly built woman, but she looked tiny perched up on a ton of Belgian. The pasture looked tiny, too, when we led Chub into it, and my two lambs suddenly looked like toys brought home to go in the baby's crib. But they were in no danger from Chub's massive feet. He ignored them completely. All that tall grass excited him, and he instantly set to work grazing. By dark he had already leveled quite a stretch—and he had also drained the lambs' drinking-tub in about six swallows, and had two refills. (We carried them from the outside faucet at the house in pails.)

66

A One-Horsepower Mower

About six-thirty Sunday morning, my wife and I were awakened by loud neighing. There is a twenty-five-acre pasture across the road from my house, and in it that morning were a number of beef cattle plus a mare named Alberta. She belongs to my neighbor Dave Chapman, another pioneer. Like Chub, she's a workhorse, though not a Belgian—she probably weighs no more than twelve hundred pounds. All day Saturday she and the cows had been out of sight, grazing back behind the big hill on the east side of the pasture. But now she was standing right across the road from Chub, whickering at him. And Chub? He was at the very front of the lamb pasture, his head, neck, and shoulders over the fence, neighing thunderously at Alberta. The fence was bowed sharply outward from his weight.

To understand all that subsequently happened, you need to know what my lamb pasture looks like. It was originally built to eliminate mowing around the vegetable garden, and it incorporates three-quarters of the garden fence. At the very front it follows a stone retaining wall about four feet high, which in turn parallels the town road. The sheep fence (woven wire, thirty-nine inches high) runs right along the top of the wall. It was here that Chub was standing, as if on the front of a stage, looking somewhat like a very large opera singer in a very small opera house. Belgians have blond manes, and specifically he looked like the biggest of all Wagnerian tenors—say, six or seven Lauritz Melchiors rolled into one.

I wasn't too worried about his jumping off the stone wall, but I *was* worried that he would dislodge a whole section of the sheep fence just by accident. The post on each side of him was creaking and groaning at that moment. I figured I had about ten minutes either to get him out or Alberta in.

Early as it was, I hurried down to Dave's, and asked him if he would lend me Alberta for a few days. Dave wasn't eager to—he seemed to feel that Alberta was quite fragile, and that Chub might hurt her—but when I explained that my fence was rocking like a ship in a storm, he finally agreed.

It worked beautifully. Chub was gentle as anything with Alberta. The two of them grazed happily side by side. Both of them being big eaters, by Sunday evening nearly half the pasture was cropped down. Apart from the fact that Chub would not let me give the lambs their daily handful of grain (acknowledging their existence for the first time, he swatted them away on each side with a swing of his head, and ate the grain himself), there were no problems at all. Unless you count filling the drinking-tub five times in one day as a problem.

Monday morning before breakfast I went out to check things and to grain the lambs. I had two coffee cans of grain with me, and a simple plan. One can I would dump into the lambs' grain dish; and while Chub was eating it, I would race to the back of the pasture, followed by the lambs, and feed them secretly behind an apple tree.

That worked, too. Chub never suspected a thing. As I strolled back from the apple tree, there he was, still licking the lambs' dish with an enormous tongue, while Alberta watched wistfully from a distance of about eight feet. Brains over brawn, I thought, pleased with myself.

Then my eye was caught by the garden fence. Most of it was leaning inward at an angle of about thirty degrees. The pasture was still nearly half covered with lush grass, but those damned horses had been all around the sides of the garden during the night, sampling produce. It was still early in June, and the corn fortunately was not up yet. They weren't interested in potato plants. But for a distance of three and a half feet every row of peas, every row of lettuce, every row of beans was eaten.

I still had an hour before I absolutely had to leave for work. Most of it I spent furiously straightening posts and tacking a strand of barbed wire along the top of the garden fence. The two horses watched with interest, but made no attempt to interfere.

When I got home that evening, the remaining vegetables were untouched. Better yet, the grass in the pasture was now two-thirds grazed down, and I figured another day or two would finish the job. I *did* note that one apple tree had lost a major limb, presumably while Chub was having a scratch—but it was a tree that needed pruning anyway, and I decided not to let myself get upset.

The decision was temporary. During dinner we heard a report like a rifle shot, and I rushed out to investigate. Cut off from his garden nibblings by the strand of barbed wire, Chub had been reaching over the big sheep-pasture gate to sample the grass outside. (It was identical to the grass inside, only shorter.) Just by resting his neck on it, he had broken the top two-by-four and twisted the whole gate. Never mind dinner; I got busy with lavish applications of barbed wire.

When we took the horses out on Tuesday evening, the pasture was as neatly trimmed as any power mower could have done—and much better fertilized. It had taken no more than five or six hours of my time, even counting the subsequent gate repairs, and I am sure I saved at least a quart of gas.

In fact, I was well enough pleased so that this year I plan

to repeat the experiment and save another quart of gas. Just two things will be different. First, I will have a strand of barbed wire around the entire pasture. People say you shouldn't use barbed wire with horses, but clearly they've never tried keeping horses in the side yard, or they wouldn't say it. Second, my visitors are going to be a couple of the smallest, oldest, and most sedate saddle horses I can find. Workhorses are glorious creatures, but as to their effect on ordinary fences, I'd rather have a Sherman tank.

On Porcupine Hill

THREE FALLS IN A ROW NOW, it's happened. I've walked out to the second sheep pasture, the small back one, to take the lambs some grain, and I've found one of them pacing miserably back and forth with his nose full of porcupine quills. There follows a ten-minute operation with a pair of pliers, about which each of the lambs has been remarkably brave. Much braver than their owner. I can hardly bear to see the quills rip out, and usually settle for holding the lamb in my arms while my wife does the pulling.

At least it's not as bad as taking quills out of a dog. Dogs, reckless enthusiasts that they are, will bound up to a porcupine and instantly try a bite. They then come weeping home with their mouths held carefully open and their tender tongues full of quills. Lambs never get quills inside their mouths.

I haven't actually seen an encounter between a lamb and a porcupine, because porcupines operate almost entirely at night. But after three years I've been able to work out with some accuracy what happens.

The lambs' back pasture is the last level piece of ground

under a steep rocky hillside. (Level for Vermont, that is. In Kansas it would probably be called Mt. Lamb, and have children sledding across it.) The hillside is full of small caves, and by day there is nearly always at least one porcupine lurking in one of them.

What happens is that some October night a porcupine happens to come down to the bottom of the hill in search of a fresh tree to destroy, and then he becomes aware that the lambs have a small salt block. The other thing that porcupines care about besides stripping trees of their bark is salt. In fact, "care" is too mild a word. It's true passion. If there were ever a society of reformed porcupines (and there wouldn't be), it would be called Salt Hogs Anonymous.

As soon as he smells that salt, the porcupine climbs one of the fence posts, eases down into the lamb pasture, and begins to waddle purposefully toward the brick. The lambs, of course, hear him coming. Meaning no harm of any sort, they gambol up to examine the new creature, sort of like flower children examining a National Guardsman. Whichever one is dominant that year puts his head down to sniff.

Whap! As soon as the lamb puts his nose down, the porcupine swings with his tail—and that's the third thing porcupines like to do: swing their tails. They have very good aim. The lamb, of course, leaps back in pain, with somewhere between ten and thirty quills in his nose and around his mouth. Both lambs now stay at a respectful distance while the porcupine plods on over to their salt block and gorges himself. And the next day I hold the victim in my arms while my wife pulls out the quills.

People claim that sheep are not very intelligent and I

concede that is mostly the case. But about porcupines they're fast learners. I've known dogs that had to meet four or five porcupines before they learned not to rush up impulsively, and I have never known a dog that learned from just one encounter. All sheep do. If only I kept a permanent flock, instead of buying new lambs every spring, it might even turn out that sheep can teach other sheep. It wouldn't surprise me a bit if last year's victim, now a yearling ram, herded the friendly youngsters away when the porcupine appeared.

If I had a permanent flock, and if the older sheep did keep curious lambs away from that deadly tail, it would diminish my hatred for porcupines. Certainly I don't begrudge their coming into the lamb pasture and taking some of the salt, if they would only leave the lambs alone.

But a permanent flock wouldn't *end* my hatred. Because at the other end of the porcupine from his spiky tail is something even worse. In fact, two things. One is a set of rodent teeth, big and sharp. The other is a mean, lazy little brain. This combination spells death to trees.

Since I also spell death for trees (I cut fifty or sixty nice ones for firewood every year), and death for lambs, too, I am in no position to be excessively critical of porcupines. But at least I don't butcher a lamb and just keep the two best lamb chops, or cut a tree and take one piece of firewood. Porcupines do that sort of thing all the time.

There used to be a stand of young sugar maples at the bottom of Porcupine Hill. There were maybe forty of them: three, four, five inches in diameter. One winter night a hungry porcupine came by. Starting with the first tree, he ate the bark off starting at snow level and going up maybe seven inches. That represents how high he could reach up without having to crink his neck or stand up on his hind legs. When he had girdled the first tree, he moved on to the second. For all I know, to the third. Then he waddled back to his cave to sleep it off. The next night he came back and started in on another. When I first noticed, he had seventeen girdled.

The little monster could, of course, have taken the trouble to stand up. That would have given him three times as much food per tree. Not that I would have been satisfied even then. Because porcupines are excellent climbers. On a big tree where the bark of the trunk is too tough and indigestible, they do in fact shinny right up and strip the branches. If he had been willing to do that with these young maples, he could have gotten more meals out of just one tree than he actually got from all seventeen that he killed. It's true that he spared the rest of the grove. But don't think he did it from some sense of environmental concern. He did it only because I succeeded in trapping him the next night at the foot of the eighteenth tree.

To be honest, I would still hate porcupines a little bit, even if they stayed away from my lambs and even if they ate whole trees. I would hate them for their salt gluttony. One fall a few years ago, we had a very early snowfall— around the seventh of November. The forecasters knew it was coming; and when I had heard the 6:00 P.M. news, so did I. After dinner I went out to the barn to put snow tires on my truck.

There was a loud scuttling noise as I approached. A very large porcupine waddled rapidly (for him) away from the corner where I kept the tires. There was some sort of black stuff on the floor through which he made tracks as he ran.

The black stuff turned out to be a couple of hundred

chips he had removed from one snow tire. There was a little road salt on that tire from the previous winter. A nicer animal might have just licked it off. Not the porcupine. He bit hunks out of the tire and, I presume, sucked them like hard candy. He hadn't had time to girdle the tire when I interrupted him, but that clearly had been his intention. I firmly believe that porcupines would girdle the highways if their teeth were just a little stronger.

All this may sound as if I think the world would be a better place with no porcupines. That's not quite true. I would be delighted to see a pair of them in every city zoo.

Postscript, 1983. Since I wrote that, a one-time Colorado rancher named David Wood has taught me a better way to get quills out than yanking with pliers. You cut a little piece off the exposed end of each quill, and dab the cut with vinegar. The quill being hollow, it soaks the vinegar right up—and rather quickly goes soft. You can then pull it out with your fingers.

I've only had to use the new technique once. Fisher-cats, I rejoice to say, have come back to Vermont; and where there are fishers, the porcupine population tends to moderate. Judging by that one lamb, the vinegar-softened quills come out quite painlessly.

Man of a Thousand Odors

THE ADS SHOW VIRILE FELLOWS swinging their soap-on-a-rope in a locker room, or standing explorer-like in a rural landscape. They give off almost visible waves of delicious scent: English Leather, or Eau Sauvage, or Acqua di Selva. An admiring and beautiful woman often stands a pace or two behind, though they ignore her. Her nostrils are slightly flared. She has clearly been following her nose to the source of this splendid masculine aroma. It is so intoxicating that she seems likely to spring from behind, and bear the man down to the grass.

I would dearly love to believe the promise of these ads. What could be more agreeable than to have a stream of beautiful women moving upwind, irresistibly drawn by the super-male scent I wear? Surely I would dab myself with Jovan Grass Oil in the morning, splash with Timberline for lunch, and fairly drench myself with Acqua di Selva as bedtime drew near.

The trouble is that I live in just such a rural landscape as the ads depict. In the course of a normal day I pick up a good many of the rough male scents they describe, not by opening a bottle but just by living. The results for me are so dramatically different from what is about to happen in the ads that I am forced to be skeptical.

Take Acqua di Selva, which calls itself "woodsy" (so is Timberline, I presume), and promises wearers that they will smell as cool and fresh as a rain forest. Two days in three I smell woodsy. We heat our house mostly with wood, and I have about ten cords a year to cut. I have a fifty-acre woodlot to cut it on—hilly, rugged terrain that would photograph well. Occasionally I even notch and fell a few sawlogs for the mill: Scotch pine, and towering spruces, and wild cherry.

Not only do no women ever follow the woodsy smell to where I am cutting, pluck the chainsaw from my hand, and lead me to a patch of ferns, my wife doesn't even let me in the house when I get home. She stops me on the front porch. Nose averted, she combs the wood chips out of my hair. Then she hands me a cake of soap, and suggests I go take a bath in the river. When, as occasionally happens, I cut on a rainy day, and hence come dripping home out of the rain forest, leaving a trail of mud and bark, she has been known to burst into tears.

The smell of leather has proved even less erotic. We have a bright bay gelding named Cinnamon, a fine riding horse. We have lots of horsy tack, and even a sort of tack room. Leather halters hang from pegs. There are lead ropes and bridles and, sitting on a rack made from wood cut on the place, a saddle of the same shape that is shown in gold silhouette on the English Leather bottle.

The fact that my wife tends to avoid me when I've been cleaning it doesn't prove anything, I admit, since the saddle was made in Japan and is presumably Japanese Leather. But the bridles are both English. And both, I will say it plainly, savor of horse sweat.

Cinnamon loves to canter, and he sweats a lot; also he champs at the bit and gets froth all over. Froth composed, of course, of horse-spit. It is true that once when I rode him to a party, a very pretty girl came out and kissed not me, but him. It is also true that she then went quickly to the bathroom and washed her hands and face.

Then there is the soil itself. Jovan Grass Oil promises to give its wearer the powerful attraction of smelling "earthy," a claim that I find the least plausible of all. I mean, for all I know, men who use Grass Oil may smell earthy, but I don't think that's going to help their social lives much.

We are gardeners. I have a generous supply of rich garden earth on my hands, under my fingernails, on my boots, etc., through most of each May and June, and all it ever gets me is the earnest plea to take my boots off outside and then head straight for the bathroom.

Once I hand-dug a well, and then I was *really* earthy. You could have planted corn on any part of me. At that time I was not married, but engaged. An engagement that never ripened into marriage, as it turned out. My fiancée's quite serious proposal was that we walk (she didn't want me in her car) to her father's house, and that she then turn the garden hose on me. "You're all over mud," she said in repelled tones.

I frankly don't think *any* male perfume is going to attract women much. They prefer us neutral—if only so as not to collide with their own fragrance. But if I were going to try perfume in a serious way, I would forget all this earthy, woodsy, leathery stuff. In fact, I would forget the whole rural bit. I would aim to have the faint, sweet smell of a single flower in a city square.

My Life as a Peasant

AT LEAST IF YOU'RE A ROMANTIC like me, it is easy
to idealize medieval life. To a modern eye, or to mine,
anyway, the very word "medieval" has a romantic aura. I
think it's that first "e." You picture all those fine harmoni-
ous scenes: the lords and ladies out on horseback with their
hawks and hounds; the plowman out with *his* horse, whis-
tling as he plows; peasants reaping the fields (and taking
luxurious naps behind the windrows); the maiden at her
carding; the walled monastery; the castle, with swans
swimming on the moat; and knights and their squires
gravely returning from the Holy Land.

One of the great appeals of those scenes is that they are
so nearly free from our vulgar obsession with cash. Everything is done in terms of barter, and service, and villeinage.
The knight pays rent to his feudal superior: each year a
fatted calf and a red rose on Lady Day. The reapers bring
in their sheaves—and use them instead of money. With a
tithe of the crop they support the priest of the little parish
church, and some sheaves probably go to the lord of the
manor. The old granny goes to market, trading eggs for
pins and trinkets. It's all so beautiful and so *physical*. Dollar

bills and credit cards are just not in it with roses and sheaves of wheat.

Lately I've had a little taste of medieval-style life, however, and it turns out I don't like it quite as well as I thought I would.

The way it happened was this. A farmer I know named Delbert Shands is one of the deacons of a country church. Besides the honor of the thing, he gets to do quite a lot of work. Most recently he found himself on a committee of three deacons assigned to cut wood for the minister. The minister used to have oil heat in the parsonage; he could just turn up the thermostat and get cracking on a sermon. (The church itself has never ceased to use wood stoves—but then it only has to be heated on Sunday.) Then last year, as fuel prices kept rising, the congregation thriftily voted to install a wood-burning furnace in the parsonage, thus returning the situation to what it was thirty years ago. It also undertook to provide free wood.

The trees the three deacons chose to cut were a row of roadside maples that had died from too much salt, which is a common fate of roadside maples these days. Beautiful wood, but hard to convert to burnable size. These were trees a century old: they averaged better than two feet in diameter, and they were full of knots. Even after limbing, each trunk weighed about three tons.

One deacon has a logging truck, and he hauled these mighty logs over and dumped them on the parsonage lawn. The second deacon, who has a chainsaw with a twenty-four-inch bar (that's huge), came and bucked them all up into furnace-length pieces. It was then my friend Delbert's job to split it all. Since he knows I have a hydraulic splitter mounted on my tractor, and since he has at various times

lent me his manure spreader, his hay conditioner, and even
his baler, he didn't have much hesitation about asking me
to come help him. You *can* split big roadside maples by
hand, if you have enough wedges, but to do a pile like that
you better figure on putting in all your spare time for a
month.

I gladly agreed to help, and it wasn't just because I owed
Del the return favor. I was also attracted by the medieval-
ness of the arrangement. I'm not a member of his church—
in fact, I'm not even sure I'm still a Christian—but the idea
of helping to split the minister's wood appealed to me very
much. Back when I was a good Episcopalian, all I ever did
for my church was to put money in the collection plate—
and, later, pledge cards, as our parish got steadily more
tax-conscious and less physical. But bringing in the winter's wood-supply . . . Even though the tractor might be a
slightly incongruous element, I could easily be part of a
marginal illustration in some thirteenth-century Book of
Hours.

I have a job that lets me take a day off when I need to,
and Del's time is pretty much his own between morning
and evening milkings. I don't mean that he's idling around;
on the contrary, he always has more work than he can do.
It's just that being his own boss, he can decide when he'll
do what. So last November we picked a Wednesday, and
met at the parsonage after milking. That is, about quarter
past eight.

It was a cold, bright morning: good working weather.
The yard was strewn with maple logs two feet in diameter
and two feet long. They were too heavy to lift and too
heavy even to roll easily. But we had thought to bring a
couple of peaveys, and with a little straining we could get

the logs onto my splitter. It was hard work, though. Despite the thirty-degree temperature, we were soon both sweating. There was no sign of life inside the parsonage; Del explained that the minister was off at a conference down in Massachusetts.

By noon we were all done but half a dozen blocks. There were three huge piles of split wood in the yard. I was ravenously hungry, and though the rest of me was sweaty, my hands were numb with cold. I was looking forward to getting those last few done, and heading home. I would still have a long, frostbitten ride on the tractor.

At this point, a shiny little car swung in front of the parsonage and stopped. A tall young man got out, followed by his wife, carrying a baby. The minister was home from the conference. He looked very urban and relaxed. As my eye traveled up him from bottom to top, I saw first the polished loafers, then the gray flannels, then the bright yellow sweater fitting nicely over his muscular shoulders. Finally his tanned face and head of dark hair. He formed quite a contrast to Delbert and me, with our sweaty work clothes and graying hair. (I must be twenty years older than the minister, and Del is ten years older than I am.)

Del's face brightened, and he sprang up to say hello. I went on splitting. They talked for a minute, or, rather, the minister talked while Del listened respectfully. Then the minister, the wife, and the baby went on into the warm house. Del came back looking slightly depressed.

" 'Fraid we're not quite done yet," he said. "He told me there's some more wood inside the garage, and I guess we better get that, too."

"Some" was an understatement. One side of the garage was packed solid with heavy maple logs. Mostly the smaller ones, but there was still a full hour's splitting in there. For the first few minutes I kept thinking, well, he'll have that yellow sweater and those loafers off, and any minute now he'll be out in his work clothes to help us. And probably she'll insist on bringing out some coffee.

But the door stayed closed. Maybe he had letters to write, or some notes from the conference to study; maybe he was just having lunch. We finished about one-twenty and left, and the door had never opened.

During the time between twelve and one-twenty, I began to get some idea of what it would have been like to be a peasant living near some thirteenth-century French monastery and doing occasional corvée labor under the watchful eye of Brother Cellarer. We may have looked good in the illuminations (doubtless made by Brother Illuminator sitting comfortably inside in yellow sandals and a clean wool gown), but we had cold hands, and no one was bringing us hot soup from the monastery kitchen. We were, in fact, mere background, like the fatted calves and the red roses.

I still like the physicalness of the Middle Ages, and especially all that barter and villeinage. But I'm clear that real peasant life is picturesque only from the outside. If I ever time-travel back to the thirteenth century, I plan to be either a prosperous city merchant or possibly one of those lords on horseback. Unless, of course, I opt to be Brother Illuminator.

Two Letters to Los Angeles

I

NOVEMBER 10, 1980—Today it snowed six times in Vermont. These are the fourth through ninth times it has snowed so far this fall.

Before you start imagining pretty white flakes drifting down, let me describe a few of today's snowfalls. The first two were mere flurries, grayish, sleety snow that didn't even stick. The third was bigger, but no more romantic. It began about 11:00 A.M. I was out in my woodlot, stacking red maple logs that I had cut and split yesterday. Promptness matters here. If I don't stack them within a day or two, they freeze to the surface and are locked in until spring.

Quite abruptly, a sharp little wind came up, and then the ground began to hiss. Snow pellets were falling thickly —not straight down from the heavens, but blown at a twenty-degree angle from the east. They didn't come hard enough to punch holes in the dead leaves, or even to sting the face much. Just hard enough to hiss against the ground.

When the squall stopped around eleven-thirty, the woods were actually rather pretty. By early November the fallen leaves have mostly lost their color—but in the right light you can still see traces of their once-glorious reds and yellows and oranges. The end of the squall produced a few thin gleams of sunlight that were the right light. Most of the woods' floor was covered with a quarter-inch layer of snow pellets, precisely that oyster color that some women seem to prefer for painted woodwork. But in the lee of each evergreen tree, and even behind the trunks of the larger maples, there was a patch of bare leaves, faintly glowing. Think of those as comparable to the windows in the oyster-colored houses. Though I was a little cold, and my leather gloves were sopping, I took an appreciative walk before I got back to stacking cordwood.

The afternoon was worse weather than the morning, at least for my purposes. Now out of the woods and back home, I was waiting for a neighbor to come and slaughter our lambs. Meanwhile, the sky had changed from alternating sun and snow to a steady, mean gray.

George arrived with his gun and his set of knives around 2:00 P.M. From then until dark, he was busy killing and skinning lambs, and I was busy salting down the hides, burying guts in the garden (terrific fertilizer), and helping him on two-person parts of the job. All of this would have been a good deal more pleasant if the temperature had not remained a constant thirty-three degrees, and if, at intervals, we hadn't got another handful of snow pellets flung in our faces. You can't skin lambs with gloves on; you can't even properly salt down hides that way.

Just before dark—that is, about twenty to five—we put

the carcasses in the back of my pickup and took them over to Enoch Hill's. Enoch lives half a mile away, and is a country butcher. About a week from now he'll return me four legs of lamb, many packages of tiny lamb chops, and more sheep kidneys, hearts, and lungs than I ever know what to do with. I was so cold by then that I went home, crammed the main stove as full of logs as it will go, and went upstairs to take a hot bath.

This, of course, is autumn. We still have winter to come. Today's bit of snow will almost certainly melt, even on the north sides of buildings. But some time two weeks or a month from now we'll get snow that means to stay. We'll have it until the end of March. When it goes, we'll have more in April—big wet snows that stick. Once in a shady cove on the river, I found snow on the fourth of May.

Why on earth does anyone choose to live here? There are known to be options, including places where November might yield a string of langorous days in the eighties.

Enoch was born here, and in that sense maybe didn't choose. (Though he could always emigrate, as a God's plenty of his forebears did. There's a steep ridge not ten miles from our village which for more than a hundred years has been called California Hill. From its top, Vermonters setting out west in their covered wagons took a last look back at the frostbitten landscape they were leaving.)

But George and I were not born here. We both came fluttering into the state like moths, drawn to the light. So what is it that draws us?

My mother used to say it was masochism. She could understand coming for the brief, lush-green summers, but a will to spend the other seasons here she could only attribute to perversity.

Myself, I think there are two quite different reasons. One depends on the well-known theory of challenge and response. If you want to have responses, the theory says, you need challenges. These our rotten climate provides. I didn't really want it to be thirty-three degrees and snowing when we dressed off the lambs. In fact, I wondered out loud to George when he arrived if it wouldn't make sense to wait for a better day. He answered like a good Vermonter that (a) there might not *be* any better day, and (b) in any case best get it done now, while the knife was sharp. And once we had done it, and even though I only assisted, I felt a little bit heroic, as if there'd been an accomplishment. To feel that is an agreeable response.

The other reason is simply the human love of variety and perhaps even of unpredictability. This love is, of course, balanced by an almost-as-strong love of sameness and predictability, which is why uniform "national" products are so reassuring, why people stay at Holiday Inns, where, when you've seen one, you've seen them all, and so forth. But love of the unpredictable is a shade stronger, strong enough, sometimes, to keep people out of paradise.

I can best illustrate that with the story of a hitchhiker I once picked up. This was during mud season, an April afternoon when it was alternately snowing and raining. I was taking the back road between two remote villages, and came on a teenage boy with his thumb out. Of course I picked him up, and of course we got into talk. He seemed strangely cheerful for a kid in a wet blue-denim jacket out hitching in such miserable weather. When I eventually asked him where he was from, he said St. Thomas.

"St. Thomas? I thought that was one of the Virgin Islands."

87

"It is."

"But don't the Virgin Islands have a perfect climate, just like Los Angeles, never too hot and never too cold, and always sunny?"

"Yes."

"Can I ask you how you happened to come to Vermont for mud season?"

"Oh," he said casually, "I just got tired of one goddamned perfect day after another."

I I

NOVEMBER 18, 1980—The tenth snow of autumn was expected to be a mere squall, like the other nine. One pessimistic forecaster said there might be an inch or two.

But when we got up this morning, there was six inches on the ground. More snow was falling fast. That's not supposed to happen before Thanksgiving—and in fact it hasn't happened in about a decade.

All the stuff that careless people like me had left outdoors was buried. There weren't even mounds to show where axes and garden hoses lay—just this smooth white sheet. It was a true winter scene. All the evergreens drooped their branches under heavy loads of snow; all the roads were salted and hideous-slushy. School was canceled in the whole region.

My neighbor Floyd and I had planned to spend the morning loading the last of his manure pile in a spreader and spreading it in the pasture that our cows share. After that we were going to store the spreader in my barn for the

winter. In the afternoon Floyd had meant to
November sawdust at the mill. (He uses it for
cows.) Me, I had meant to buck up a big ash log
of our shared pasture, split it, load it, and deliver it to a
firewood customer in the next village. It was one I had cut
in the spring, and leaf-dried.

Naturally all these plans got changed. Floyd makes part
of his winter-living plowing driveways. Before dawn he
spent an hour mounting his plow, and was on the road in
time to plow out people who leave for work at seven. Then
he did the morning milking and went out to plow again.
I spent half an hour feeling around in the snow with my
boot toes for tools. (I found them all.) I brought in a lot of
snow-covered wood for the stove, and fed the beef cattle.
Finally, around nine o'clock, I trudged into the woods to
rescue my tractor. I had it parked about half a mile off the
road.

That's not quite as foolish a place to keep it as it sounds.
In fact, it's a very sensible place. Every year when we're
finished cutting hay—this ought to be early July, but is
more usually around the first of September—I take the
mowing machine off. Then I mount a hydraulic wood-
splitter on the back and wiggle the tractor into whatever
part of the woods I'm thinning that year. It stays there
until just before I think we'll have serious snow.

I was lucky. Even though the snow was now seven
inches deep, and getting more serious by the minute, the
tractor wiggled back out of the woods without getting stuck
even once. Because I didn't dare take either hand off the
wheel, I did get a few facefuls of snow, passing under
hemlocks with especially low-drooped branches, but that
was a cheap price for getting the tractor safely out.

What I should have done was take it right home, drive it into the barn, and mount my own snowplow blade. Then plow out my barnyard. But the ease with which I had wiggled through half a mile of woods made me overconfident—besides, there's a certain thrill to taking risks. What I actually did was drive straight to the pasture and over to that big ash log. I lowered the splitter near the butt end of it. Then I walked back out on the tracks, got my truck and chainsaw, and drove them in, too. Two hours later I had half a cord of beautiful ash firewood neatly stacked in the back of the truck. Meanwhile, the snow had begun to taper off (there was just under nine inches on the ground), and the temperature had risen to a couple of degrees above freezing.

I thought I'd take the truck out first. It's four-wheel-drive and quite nimble. Even though the pasture is a very old one, and you enter it through a little curving lane lined with granite posts that some farmer quarried on the place around 1800, I didn't see why I couldn't boom on out. The heavy load would make for beautiful traction.

And so it would have, except for the unfortunate matter of its having got so warm. Snow at thirty-four degrees Fahrenheit, lying on frozen grass, makes something close to a friction-free surface. I did get halfway up the lane. I might even have made it if the truck hadn't begun to side-slip right into a granite post eight inches by eight inches and five feet tall. There was nothing to do but stop and get out.

A few years ago I would have panicked. I would have unloaded all the wood, right there in the snow. I would have walked home and gotten the kind of hand winch that we call a come-along. Then I would have spent the rest of the afternoon hand-winching. No one wants to have his truck and tractor trapped out in the pasture from mid-November until sometime in April.

But there are a few advantages to our climate, and one is that you can always count on it to get colder again. What I actually did was go do other things, and wait for dark. By 6:00 P.M. the temperature was well below freezing and the snow nicely crisped up. Truck and tractor came briskly on out—and their headlights on the untrodden pasture snow even had a kind of beauty.

At six-thirty I came crunching into the yard of my customer. He's a newcomer from the city, a former New York accountant who's been accounting in Vermont for just a couple of years. For that reason I called ahead to see if he really wanted his last load of wood to arrive on a snowy evening. Customers are expected to help unload.

"Sure, why not?" he'd said casually. "Wait any longer, and the cellar doors may be buried."

He was waiting by the open bulkhead—off which, of course, he had just shoveled nine inches of snow. We began to pitch the wood down. I was wearing thermal boots, and overalls over my pants, and a wool jacket, and leather gauntlets. Snow-covered wood does get to feeling cold. But though he, too, had boots and a jacket, he hadn't bothered with gloves. With his white accountant's hands he gripped those icy logs and pitched them down cellar as lightly as if he'd been tossing grapefruits.

"I've got another pair of gloves in the truck," I said after a minute. "You want to borrow them?"

"Oh, hell, no," he said. "It's only half a cord. And the weather's not very cold, anyway."

If this is how a city accountant behaves after two years, what will he be like after ten? Probably be getting sore if we don't have frosts in July. As for southern Californians, if any of them ever move here I firmly expect to see them riding down the hills on their surfboards, snow spraying up on both sides, dressed just as they would be at Hermosa Beach. Floyd and I will watch respectfully. But we won't join them.

The Gourmet Potato Grower

IN THE SPRING OF 1982, I began collecting seed potatoes for what was to be a systematic experiment. I have
grown many kinds of potatoes over the past twenty years,
but never systematically. It was always two or three varieties one year, two or three the next, as neighbors happened to give me a handful of seed potatoes, or as my eye
was caught by a new (to me) variety in the feed store. And
that made sense. Who, other than agronomists, needs more
than two or three kinds? Potatoes aren't like Bordeaux
wines, or even like apples, where a new variety can provide
a dazzling experience for the palate. Potatoes operate
within a narrow flavor range. There are even people who
think that when you've tasted one, you've tasted them all.

These people are, of course, mistaken. In their quiet
way, potatoes do differ. And for several years I have been
getting increasingly curious about how much distinction a
moderately attentive person can in fact make between one
kind and another. Maybe I was nudged an extra bit by
reading that in eighteenth-century Japan farmers were
growing more than a thousand varieties of rice. I think of
rice as having an even narrower flavor band than potatoes.

Another nudge came from the accident of taking a trip. Usually I just stay home in Vermont and tend my farm. But in the spring of 1982 I happened to be making a tour that would take me to South Dakota, Nebraska, Kansas, and Missouri. Here was a chance, I thought, to pick up the potatoes of another region. We have our Kennebec, Katahdin, and Green Mountain white—really tan—potatoes here: two varieties associated with Maine, and one with Vermont itself. Less common, but still readily for sale, we have Pontiacs, which are a red-skinned variety, Red Norlands, and occasionally Russet Burbanks. And finally we have one or two obscure local varieties that you never find in a store at all, such as Cow Horns. Cow Horns have dark purple skin, and are the curious shape that their name implies. I figured there would be an identical situation in the Midwest, only with an all-different cast. I was so sure of it that I took an extra suitcase along just for bringing back my Midwestern potatoes.

As it turned out, I barely needed space in a flight bag. My first stop was Rapid City, South Dakota. When the people I was visiting took me to a farm supply store, I was astonished to see that what they stocked were Katahdins, Kennebecs, Pontiacs, and Russet Burbanks. I could just as well have been in White River Junction, Vermont.

Had it been celery or carrot seed I was after, I might have expected this. I knew that the seed business went national some time ago—caught up in the same frenzy of standardization and mass marketing that makes the shelves of a supermarket in Denver almost identical to those of a supermarket in Boston, or that has closed all but a few dozen local breweries, so that beer tastes the same coast to coast. For that matter, I knew that Harris Seed is merely a division of the Celanese Corporation, that Scott and Burpee are both owned by ITT, and so on.

But I supposed that potatoes would be exempt. You don't buy seed, you buy the whole potato—and when our local farm supply man in Vermont gets his seed potatoes in, his usual order is seven tons. That seems a little heavy for it all to be coming out of a few ITT warehouses.

My total haul from the Midwest was a kind of red potato called Viking. I got it in the Earl May store (one of a chain) in the little town of Nebraska City. And along with it I got another lesson in the ingenuity of conglomerates—and maybe one also in the sheeplike docility of us consumers. There were no seven tons of seed potatoes clogging the Earl May store in Nebraska City. Instead there were a lot of dainty plastic packages, each containing fifty pre-cut eyes.

It cost me $3.50 for one packet of Viking eyes, which is something like five times as much as actual potatoes yielding fifty eyes would cost. And since there's just a little button of potato with each eye, your crop is off to a slower start. But it sure does save some big corporation a lot of shipping costs. And anyway, I was probably lucky to find even one new kind. I have since learned that seventy-three percent of all the potatoes grown in the United States belong to just four varieties. So much for regionalism.

When I got off the plane with my empty second suitcase and my little packet of eyes, I had a grand total of seven kinds of potatoes. That was in mid-April. A month later, when I planted, I put in fifteen varieties. Seven of the other eight came from a single farm about twenty miles away from mine. I'd been over to the feed store in Chelsea, which is our county seat, and was grumbling to the proprietor that all he ever had was Kennebecs, Green Mountains, Katahdins, etc. He heard me out, and then said, "If I was you, I'd go over to Harold Hayward's place." I did, and came home with Early Roses, Red Roses, Buttes, Superiors, Bonnie Blue Eyes, Blue Victors—and best of all, some of the Cow Horns I'd been vainly scouring the countryside for. I'd also seen Mr. Hayward's numerous potato ribbons from the Tunbridge Fair.

The eighth I got from a man in West Fairlee who was fixing my roof. Bob Adams is a gardener of considerably greater ingenuity than I am; and from time to time he amuses himself by taking one of the seedballs that occasionally appear on mature potato vines and growing a crop from scratch. You get a disorderly mix of wild potatoes if you do this, which is why potatoes aren't sold as seed. Bob raised about twenty kinds of potatoes from one seedball a few years ago, most of them quite unattractive. He saved samples of the best six to plant the next year. Then he cut down to three, and finally to the handsome tan potato which he had not bothered to name until he gave me five pounds of them in April, 1982. Then, at my request, he did. The fifteenth and rarest variety of potato I grew is called Adams's Delight. You won't find one in the whole state of Idaho, still less in any of Earl May's stores.

By the first of June I had all fifteen varieties planted, maps drawn to show which were where, and (not completely trusting my maps) poles laid on the ground to outline each of the fifteen beds. Eight varieties were mulched, and seven were not. This was to test the claim of another neighbor that potato bugs tend to stay away from mulched vines. I couldn't see that they did. I did see very clearly, though, that gourmets among potato bugs prefer the tender tops of Cow Horns. There were days when I'd pick thirty potato bugs off the Cow Horn vines, and find maybe ten more in the whole rest of the patch.

About the first of October I began to harvest. My daughters, who generally avoid the vegetable garden, helped. Digging potatoes has enough in common with looking for buried treasure to excite even blasé teenagers, and we got the whole crop dug in two afternoons. The yields varied enormously. In some cases, such as Bonnie Blue Eyes, Mr. Hayward had only three or four potatoes that he could spare. Furthermore, I got dreadfully behind on my weeding in August, and one result of *that* was that a lot of the unmulched potatoes were the size of hen's eggs. But there remained sufficient of each kind for numerous test meals.

It is not easy to compare fifteen varieties of potatoes with each other. In fact, it's extremely hard. Once cooked, most tan potatoes look pretty much alike, even with their skins on. So do most reds. If you were going to serve fifteen kinds of boiled new potatoes at the same meal, you'd have to boil them in twelve or thirteen pots to preserve their identity. (Cow Horns and a couple of others are still spottable when cooked.) Who has a stove that big? I wound up doing the tests in relays.

I also wound up with conclusive findings. For boiled potatoes, roast, baked, and many others. Except maybe in stew, where the gravy and the onions overwhelm all other flavors, a moderately attentive person can make distinctions with no trouble at all.

Take the case of fried potatoes. This is a particularly interesting case, because the commonest way Americans now encounter potatoes is in an order of fries at Mc-

Donald's or Wendy's. That means they are eating Russet Burbanks, probably from Idaho, as they would also be at Burger King.

Russet Burbanks are far and away the most widely eaten potato in America, accounting for forty percent of consumption all by themselves. (Kennebecs, much used in commercial potato chips, Katahdins, and Sebagoes are the other big three.) They enjoy this distinction in part because of their shape. Being naturally shaped somewhat like oval bars of bath soap, they can be cut up for French fries with much less waste than a roundish potato like a Katahdin or a Viking. They can also stand a good deal of freezing and processing—and a fast-food-chain potato had better be able to tolerate that.

I began the fried potato tests at a lunch for two: just my elder daughter and me. Trying for a gamut, we picked six varieties: Russet Burbank, of course; Adams's Delight and Butte, which are respectively a tan potato and another russet; Bonnie Blue Eyes, a very pale tan potato with a purple-bluish aureole around each eye; Red Rose, the handsomest of all the red potatoes; and Cow Horns. We sliced them as you would cucumbers, got out six frying pans, and proceeded to make home fries. We used fresh bacon grease from our own pig.

All six kinds were good, which is what you'd expect, since the dominant impressions of a fried potato are crispness, greasiness, and saltiness, with the potato itself a mere vehicle. But all were not equally good. We ruled out Cow Horns right away. Poor texture. Then we eliminated Red Rose, Adams's Delight, and Russet Burbank as being about equally pleasant, but nothing special. That left Butte, which had a faint but distinct nutty flavor, and Bonnie Blue

Eyes, which had a slightly different and slightly stronger nutty flavor. We both confidently called it best.

A couple of days later, three Dartmouth students came out to the farm for Sunday lunch. The menu: homemade sausage and home-fried potatoes, followed by pancakes and homemade maple syrup. (After that we drove fence posts, a high-energy job.) This time just four of our six frying pans came out. I introduced two new varieties: Pontiac, which is a red; and Blue Victor, a quite remarkable potato with dark blue skin and bright purple flesh. And I repeated Adams's Delight from the so-so group and Bonnie Blue Eyes as the winner of the first heat. Naturally I said nothing to the students about the previous tasting.

The students easily ranked all four. Adams's Delight came lowest, then Pontiac. These judgments were unanimous. On the other two there was a split. Two of the students put Blue Victor first and Bonnie Blue Eyes second; the third reversed that order. It was still blue potatoes all the way. A theory began to form itself.

A few days after that I had dinner with a friend in town and her two children. The meal included four kinds of potatoes, supplied by me and pan-fried by Janet. There were Blue Victors and Russet Burbanks as carry-overs, and two new kinds: Green Mountain and Kennebec.

My blue-potato theory instantly collapsed. Janet and both her children ranked the Blue Victors last. The taste was too strong and too earthy, they said. And what they ranked first was none other than Russet Burbanks, suggesting that maybe McDonald's, Burger King, and Wendy's are onto something after all. I had taken it for granted that they weren't onto anything, except the American fondness for uniformity. After all, I had been in touch with all three corporations. I knew that all three got their potatoes, including those served in the remotest corners of New England or Appalachia, from just three states: Idaho, Oregon, and Washington. (No wonder American energy consumption is so high—that's how we do most things.) I knew that even within those states they tended to buy from just a handful of giant agribusiness firms—in the case of Mc-Donald's, just two whopper companies, so to speak. And I knew that only Wendy's had ever even *tested* any other variety of potato. McDonald's and Burger King prefer to use their ingenuity on patenting endless tiny modifications of ways to freeze and process the same old Russet Burbanks.

So it was a shock to find this totally commercial potato coming out first in a free test.

My response was to start over. Only instead of cooking home fries, I would do deep-frying, just as if I were a Burger King franchise myself. (That would make me, incidentally, a subsidiary of the Pillsbury Company.) I would try all fifteen varieties at once. And I would assemble as many people as my kitchen table can seat.

A week later nine people sat around that table. We included two farmers, a musician, a country doctor, a cabinetmaker, a physical therapist, and three children. Most of us had grown potatoes at one time or another. All of us considered ourselves good judges of food.

For two hours we tucked into French fries, intermingling just enough steak and salad to keep our palates fresh. There was a decent Côte du Rhône for the grown-ups, homemade cider for the children. And as we ate, we kept score, on the traditional scale of one to ten.

When we were done, my blue-potato theory was demolished completely. Blue Victors placed thirteenth, Bonnie Blue Eyes a dead last. What I myself persisted in calling a nutty flavor, everyone else found earthy or even musty. Even I found them less attractive deep-fried than pan-fried; Blue Victors ranked sixth on my personal list, poor Bonnie Blue Eyes way down.

As for the winners, they were Green Mountain and Adams's Delight, both tans; the big russet named Butte; the beautiful red called Red Rose . . . and Russet Burbanks. These five stood out clearly from the rest: for texture, for distinctive but varied potato flavor, for absence of aftertaste, for ability to keep their flavor as they cooled. Jonathan, the doctor's nine-year-old son, impressed everyone when he took his first bite of Russet Burbank, knowing only that this was the eighth kind of French fry he'd tried that night, and sang out, "Hey, these are what we get at McDonald's!"

All of us agreed that we had eaten too many potatoes at one sitting. After the first ten or eleven varieties, it was a downright chore to go on, no matter how diligently we refreshed ourselves with tiny bites of steak and tiny sips of wine. If it weren't that the fifteenth and final variety we tried instantly became one of the two top winners, we might not even have trusted our jaded palates. Even as it was, we decided that for real accuracy we should have a fry-off at a later date, using only the five finalists.

The nine of us therefore met again in two weeks—this time with a home-grown ham, a Spanish white wine, and more cider. We got absolutely conclusive results. The rankings weren't identical with those of the first test, but they were close. Green Mountain was top potato then; it remained top potato now. Smooth and crisp at the same time; distinctive but not overwhelming flavor. Red Rose had been in third place before; it climbed to second now—a very strong second. Collectively we gave it seventy-eight points, while Green Mountain had seventy-nine. Butte dropped to third, with sixty-four points; Russet Burbank and Adams's Delight stayed fourth and fifth respectively, with sixty-two and sixty.

These are, of course, only the French-fry standings, and they do not apply to potatoes cooked other ways. If you boil new potatoes, you get quite different results. Pontiac, one of the red varieties, makes an exceptional boiled potato, so smooth and creamy that you don't even need salt and butter (though they taste even better if you do use them). Adams's Delight are about as good, and so, if you like a distinctive flavor, are Cow Horns.

When I got an English family in the next village to steam five varieties of potatoes in the classical English way, they put Green Mountains first. "I'd eat one even without meat and gravy," the husband reported, making it clear that this was a privilege he very seldom accorded a potato. Since Pontiac wasn't in the selection I gave them, I don't know how it would have compared. I do know that another red variety, the Vikings from Nebraska, came in second on their list, and Adams's Delight third. Blue Victors *tasted* okay steamed, they said, but the purple color put them off quite a lot, and they ranked it fourth. Superior they found a real clinker: no flavor, and the texture of soap.

Disappointing steamed, Superiors make a fine baked potato, though. Nice crumbly texture, superb flavor. In an eight-person test, using five varieties, they came in second only to Adams's Delight. Kennebecs were last—though even they made good eating, the testers said.

As for roast potatoes, Butte was most often the winner until the very last test we ran. Then my neighbor Garrett Hack, a longtime grower and lover of potatoes, spoiled everything. He brought a sack containing a new, sixteenth variety, a nameless red potato he got some years ago from a farmer up in Groton, Vermont. Matched against Buttes, the nameless reds came out ahead. Flushed with triumph, Garrett promptly named them Red Wonders. He is giving me some to grow next year. I can hardly wait to try them steamed.

What does all this prove? Two things, I think. One is that practically everybody, including small children, has gourmet potential, at least when it comes to potatoes. The housewife who grabs a sack of "Maine potatoes" or "Idaho potatoes" or "Long Island potatoes" in the supermarket is missing a treat. She could be demanding Green Mountains to fry or steam, or Buttes to roast, or Pontiacs to boil. She wouldn't be risking making her family fat, either, since, pound for pound, potatoes have about the same number of calories as fresh pears. It's the sour cream and butter that have the calories—and if you're eating gourmet potatoes, you don't need much of that stuff.

Furthermore, she would be providing something healthy as well as tasty. The great potato authority of the twentieth century (on everything except flavor, which like most scientists he ignored) was Dr. Redcliffe Salaman, for many years director of the Potato Virus Research Station in Cambridge, England. In his magisterial book, *The History and Social Influence of the Potato*, Dr. Salaman said flatly, if you want good teeth, eat potatoes. Among his evidence for that claim was a study he made of the islanders of Tristan da Cunha at a time when they lived principally on potatoes—

and never brushed their teeth. (Or, as he put it in sober academese, "It is of interest that cleansing of the teeth is neither taught nor practiced.")

Americans have much more access to sugar than Tristan da Cunhans did; and I don't think Dr. Salaman would claim for a second that *we* could switch to a potato diet, give up brushing our teeth, and nevertheless 98 percent of us would reach the age of forty without any cavities and 93 percent of us go our whole lives without any. He certainly does claim that potatoes belong in the class of virtuous rather than of sinful foods. To which I add, get the right kinds and they nevertheless taste sinfully good.

The other thing all these tests and fry-offs show is that fast-food chains are missing a bet. There they all are tied to the Russet Burbank, a good potato but hardly the top potato. The chains compete fiercely with each other, but only on inessentials, like how many ounces of ground beef to put into otherwise remarkably similar hamburgers. Like those other fierce competitors, the manufacturers of cigarettes, the big beer companies, and the makers of laundry detergents, they specialize in distinctions without much difference. Such as: our Russet Burbanks are better than your Russet Burbanks. Whereas if one of the chains were to get up its nerve and buy a few thousand tons of Green Mountains or Red Roses, their fries might actually *be* better. At the very least, they would be giving us sheeplike consumers a choice.

But such a purchase is not at all likely. No one is more conservative than a giant corporation: it has so much invested in whatever it's doing now. So I have a suggestion. Try growing a few rows of Green Mountains or Red Roses yourself next year. *That's* no work. Once you've harvested, most good food processors will convert a potato into French-fry shapes in a few seconds. Frying is a snap, and eating a delight. Put some ketchup on the table, and you might even lure a few teenagers back home for dinner. For that matter, get hold of some Red Wonders, and you might even turn them into gardeners.

Birth in the Pasture

MY FARM (THE HOUSE EXCEPTED) used to be exclusively male. It was sort of like those Greek monasteries on Mount Athos where even the cat is a tom and the chickens are roosters. Only with me it wasn't ideological, and it didn't last as long.

Female animals were excluded from the twenty monasteries on Mount Athos under a constitution promulgated in the year 1045, and still in effect now. The idea was, I think, to be even holier than other monasteries. Female animals tended not to appear on my farm between 1963 and 1974, and there was no idea at all. There was simply a timid owner who didn't want to winter livestock. It was fun to raise lambs and calves, and to see them grazing in the fields all summer. No fun (so I thought) to have to feed and water the creatures all winter. So I bought young stock every spring, and either sold or butchered in the fall.

This naturally meant that I bought males. Females are the important sex biologically—Mount Athos wouldn't last very long without the rest of Greece to supply it with monks, cats, etc.—and farmers like to keep their ewe lambs and heifer calves to raise themselves. They are delighted to sell the surplus nine-tenths of their ram lambs and bull calves.

So always excepting the house, it was just us boys on the place. And an ever-changing group of us, too, all but me.

Then one year I realized I didn't want to keep farming in this stop-and-start fashion. I wanted continuity, familiar faces in the barn, some sense of growth. In short, I wanted a year-round farm, and I wanted it badly enough to be a winter servant to livestock. Rather soon thereafter I owned my first heifer calf. Life has been getting steadily richer ever since.

That calf grew up to be a mostly Hereford cow named Michelle. (The females in the house named her.) When she was one and a half, she met her first bull, an older part-Hereford with no name and no manners. He had a long orange penis, though, and knew just how to use it. There in her own pasture Michelle became pregnant.

Mine is a generation that has wanted to be in delivery rooms. Our fathers took our mothers to hospitals, and there surrendered them to masked obstetricians. They themselves sat meekly in waiting rooms. When all the drama had taken place, behind closed doors, they might be permitted to see the new son or daughter through a glass window. Birth was a mystery to men.

My generation wanted to change that, and did. I was present in the delivery room of a humanistic hospital when my elder daughter was born. I was in the big upstairs bedroom at home, helping Dr. Putnam with the delivery —or possibly just getting in the way—when the younger one arrived. What's certain is that I was able to bring my southern wife a bottle of Dr. Pepper fourteen minutes after Amy was born. I liked that.

Seeing how eager men have been to make their way back into the human birth ceremony, it is not too surprising that some of us also want to assist at the birthings on a farm, or at least be present. Certainly I wanted to be around for the arrival of the first calf to be born on my farm in my time.

I knew the arrival date quite accurately. Michelle and the bull had gotten things started on November sixteenth, just after lunch. The gestation period in cows is about the same as in people, or a shade longer. You figure 285 days. The calf would therefore be due around August twenty-eighth. I say "around," but being an almost mystical believer in animal powers, I really expected her to hit the precise date.

The first step was to make sure I'd be here. As far as daytime went, there was no problem; in late August I'm nearly always home doing farm work anyway. But evenings are trickier. This is the last moment before summer people leave—at least, those with kids in school. They are feeling nostalgic and social. My wife and I usually get asked out as much during the second half of August—say, three or four times—as in all of September and October put together. It's kind of fun.

But first things first. We agreed that we'd accept no invitations for Delivery Day. And to leave a comfortable margin of safety, none for the day on either side.

The next step was to keep Michelle accessible. Early in August I began taking her a scoop of grain every morning, with the idea of encouraging her to hang around the front of the pasture, where I could watch her. This had its tricky aspects, too, since it's a great big pasture, and there were fourteen other cattle in with her. (One was mine; thirteen belonged to a real farmer.) All fourteen were as fond of grain as she, and at least six were her superiors in herd rank. It was not easy to make the snack an exclusive for her. But I mostly did.

What I wanted was about a two-minute period each morning when Michelle was wholly concentrated on eating, and I could examine her. Hence grain. Cows are so passionately attached to the stuff that they will permit their owners almost any liberty, from putting a rope around their necks to looking under their tails, while they are consuming it. The latter was what I wished to do.

Michelle stayed right on schedule. She had sprung bag way back on the fifteenth. Now her udder got even fuller. On the twenty-sixth of August, two of her teats were stiff with milk. On the morning of the twenty-seventh, all four were. No dilation when I looked under her tail, though. A cinch for the twenty-eighth, I thought.

But the twenty-eighth came and went, and Michelle showed no signs of going into labor. We meanwhile missed one of the perhaps two large parties a year that occur in town. No sign on the twenty-ninth. Finally, on the morning of the thirtieth, something began to happen. Michelle, who up to now had comported herself like any other cow, began to walk quite slowly and stiffly. My neighbor Floyd, who has known cows about forty years longer than I have, attributed this to overindulgence in pasture apples—no connection at all with the pregnancy, he said. But I had seen my wife walk the same way; I was sure it presaged labor.

Still, no dilation when I did my morning tail-check. None after lunch. That evening, though, just before my wife and I were supposed to be going out for the first time in a week, I noticed Michelle moving stiffly and heavily away from the herd. It is well known that cows like to be alone when they deliver. I dashed over, clean shirt and all, and found her partially dilated.

It was a dinner party we were going to, in another town, seven miles away. I found I didn't have the nerve to call my hostess and explain that I preferred to stay home and watch a cow. If Michelle had already started labor, I might have—but it could be another six hours before she did that. I resigned myself to missing the show, and to meeting a very young calf next morning.

Next morning I couldn't find either Michelle or the new calf. Ten of the thirteen other cattle were grazing quietly in the best part of the pasture—the rich, level section in front. Three were hanging around a section of fence further back, where my land adjoins Ellis Paige's, and doing some mutual head-and-neck licking over the fence with his Angus steers. But no trace of Michelle, even though I walked to the very back corner, where the pasture turns into pine trees on low ridges, with grassy glades in between.

About 8:00 A.M. I was plodding back toward the road, rather worried, and met Floyd walking briskly out. He likes births, too. Having just finished his morning milking, he was coming over to see how Michelle handled her first delivery. (He *knew* how I'd handle any medical emergencies: ineptly. That may even be one reason he came over.)

Floyd cheered me right up. In a rolling pasture like mine, he said, and especially one where there are lots of trees and bushes and glacial boulders the size of delivery trucks, you can sometimes spend half a day finding a cow that wants to hide.

We began a systematic search, walking fifty feet apart, like a couple of corvettes hunting a submarine in tandem. About eight-thirty, the senior corvette made contact.

"There's your calf," said Floyd, pointing to a white spot on one of the pine ridges. "She's got it hid in them pines."

But as we walked quietly closer, it turned out to be a single white birch hidden among the pines; the sun was lighting up a patch of bark just about the size of a Hereford's head. We resumed patrol.

By nine o'clock we had searched the whole pasture except Bill Hill. Bill Hill is on the eastern side; it's about two hundred feet high, and practically vertical. There's maybe an acre of good pasture up on top.

I hadn't even considered looking up there, because I took it for granted that a 287-day pregnant cow would not be able to climb up, especially when she's got a dilated uterus and stiff legs. But there's nowhere else *to* look. We now clamber up, Floyd in the lead.

The pasture fence runs parallel to the top of Bill Hill, slightly down on the far side, and there are several bushy little glades right along the fence line. In one of these Michelle is lying. It's about as private a delivery room as you could ask for, and delivery has just begun. Michelle has already passed the water sack that helped to dilate her, and she is having contractions about every three minutes. Each time she does, we can see two tiny light-colored spots appear. They are baby hooves.

All this we have been watching from a safe distance— thirty yards, I'd guess. Floyd now wants to get closer, to make sure those are the front hooves we're seeing. They'd better be. If they're the rear, we'll have to try to reach in and turn the calf. Otherwise there's a high risk it will be stillborn, since the umbilical cord will break before it emerges and can start breathing. Very quietly we move toward Michelle's glade. She watches us.

When we get halfway, she heaves herself to her feet. Still

walking in that slow, arthritic way (it *is* labor, not too many apples), she lumbers about a hundred feet down the fence line, and stands there looking at us. After five minutes, when we have come no closer, she lies down again in another little glade.

This time we circle around the top of the hill and come over the crest directly above her. We are within thirty feet, but shielded by a clump of fire thorns. She seems not to notice.

Another contraction, and the little dots appear. At this distance even I can recognize them as hooves, but it is still impossible to tell which pair they are. I am bitterly regretting that I didn't have the sense to shut the barway between the front and the back pastures last night before we went to the party. If I had, this scene would be taking place somewhere in the level front part. Suppose those are the rear hooves, and we wind up having to call Dr. Webster. He isn't going to be thrilled at the prospect of treating a patient on top of Bill Hill.

The contractions are beginning to show results. The little hooves now come out a couple of inches each time, and they remain visible between contractions. That happens five times. Michelle must be exhausted, because now she simply stops the whole process for about ten minutes, and rests. Chalk up one for instinctive animal powers.

Then there is a powerful contraction, and we see something white. A calf's nose! Those *are* the front hooves, and all is well. Another minute, and the whole head is out. Michelle rests briefly again, and then with a second powerful contraction pushes the calf halfway out.

At this minute Floyd gets up from where we are sitting quietly behind the fire thorn and starts walking directly toward her. "Floyd! You'll make her get up again," I hiss.

"Want to," he says, and keeps going. Slowly, but straight at her.

When he's about ten feet away, Michelle finishes bearing the calf with one mighty contraction, gets up, and backs away. We can now see that it's a bull calf (the females in the house will later name him Armand) with dark red curly hair. Already at birth he has a bull neck and the big clumsy ankles of a Hereford. He's charming and babyish—though a big baby, eighty pounds at least—but the only thing about him you'd call *delicate* is his little white head.

Floyd, still walking slowly, comes right up to Armand, who is now about thirty seconds old. He is lying just as he was born, his whole effort concentrated on trying to breathe. Not too successfully: he is rattling and wheezing. In my own childhood, human babies got spanked under these circumstances. What Floyd does is pluck a handful of dry grass, wipe the mucus from Armand's nostrils, and then knead his chest. The calf begins to breathe normally. He is one minute old.

We are not the only visitors who have been watching this birth. As Floyd turns to get another handful of grass, a series of dark spots appears on the little white head. Flies. Five of them. You'd think they might have given him one free hour, but that's not the sort of thing that occurs to flies.

Floyd has his new handful of grass. He quickly dries the calf's body, and then steps back to where I am. We watch anxiously to see if Michelle, that young and totally inexperienced mother, will own her child. Meanwhile, Armand takes his first independent action. He shakes his head briskly, and the flies depart. The motion attracts his mother, who comes over and begins to lick his rear end. God bless instinct. It's true she started at the wrong end—

she should have begun with the head, and thus cleaned his nostrils—but this is still owning. At about the second lick, Armand moos for the first time—a soft baby moo—and Michelle answers. A few more licks and he has a bowel movement. He is four minutes old.

Michelle continues to ply her tongue, and as I watch I begin to understand that old phrase about licking something into shape. She is working gradually up toward his chest, and clearly it makes him feel good. He gives a little grunt, pushes with his front legs, and tries to stand up. He makes it halfway. But he hasn't learned how to coordinate all four legs at once yet, and he instantly falls down again. Michelle keeps licking.

By now it is ten-thirty, and Floyd and I both have a day's work ahead. And I, like the flies, am ready for breakfast. But we would like to see the calf on his legs. We decide to wait a few more minutes. Armand tries twice more to get up and twice more falls down. On the fourth attempt, he makes it. The general rule is that a healthy calf ought to be up within an hour. Armand has done it in twenty-six minutes. It takes him only two minutes more to find his mother's udder. All is well; Floyd and I start down the hill.

That afternoon, the entire human population of the farm —four people—climbs up the hill. The little glade where the birth took place is empty. There's not even a trace of the afterbirth, which Michelle has obviously eaten, as cows are supposed to. We go further back along the hill, my daughter Elisabeth in the lead. Suddenly she gives a cry of triumph. There in a thicket of young poplars is the calf, standing with his legs splayed out, perfectly motionless. Michelle is nowhere in sight. Presumably she's off grazing, and has hidden her son here, leaving him orders to stay perfectly still. *How* a cow conveys such an order, no one knows, but there is no doubt that she can.

Elisabeth tiptoes up and pats the small white head. The calf rolls his eyes, but otherwise stays perfectly motionless. "You darling thing," Elisabeth says. "I think I'm going to call you Armand."

Our farm is now a farm.

Part III

Class Struggle in the Woods

AMERICANS ARE NOTORIOUSLY hard to divide along class lines. With the exception of professors of sociology (who know exactly where in the upper middle class they fit) and a few billionaires—who hope they are upper-class, but have a horrible fear there may be a real aristocracy hiding somewhere in Boston or Philadelphia—most of us have only the vaguest idea what class we belong to.

American sports are notoriously even harder to classify than most activities. I mean more than the obvious fact that rich and poor rub shoulders at baseball games, or that a carload of Cornell professors may turn up at a quite grubby boxing match, having driven four hours to get there. I mean that even where myth says there is a distinction, it won't stand up under examination. Myth says, for example, that people with yachts are upper-class and people with motorboats aren't. Myth is full of it. The board of directors of any large corporation is likely to contain some old poop who owns a yacht and another old poop who is commodore of a power squadron. Sometimes it's even the same old poop at different stages of his career. Similarly, one and the same lower-income family on the Maine coast is likely enough to own both a little motorboat and a little sailboat.

There is one exception to all this camaraderie. At least there is in New England. The two winter sports of snowmobiling and cross-country skiing split along class lines so sharply that if I were a sociologist engaged in classifying some little town in Massachusetts or Vermont, I wouldn't even bother to study residence patterns or sexual habits. I'd just wait for winter. Then I'd hang around in the woods and see who came humping by on skis and who roared past on a snow machine. I could divide that town in one day, provided snow conditions were good.

Why cross-country skiing and snowmobiling reflect class lines so perfectly is not easy to figure out. Certainly it is not a conscious act of group loyalty. No one says, "Hm, I run the town dump, so I'd better get a snow machine," or "Well, I *was* a Wellesley drop-out; I need some knickers and a pair of Finnish touring skis."

It is tempting to think it must have something to do with instant gratification versus patience and discipline. After all, what is supposed to characterize middle-class behavior is the ability to defer pleasure. Give a lower-class type a thousand dollars, and he blows it in three days, the theory goes; whereas if you give a middle-class person the thousand, he invests it at fourteen percent. Then six months later he blows the interest. (Unless he's *really* committed to bourgeois values, in which case he waits thirty-five years, and then spends the interest on the interest.)

But that won't wash. It's true enough that you can leap on a snowmobile as a total novice and vroom right off, while the technique of cross-country takes some acquiring. But it's also true that the snowmobiler may be a devoted pool player as well, and he devoted plenty of time to learning *that*. Or he may have put in hundreds or even thousands of hours practicing basketball shots, punting technique, you name it, all in hopes of future glory. Some other principle is at work.

Could it be the well-known theory of compensation? This says that the poor, leading relatively powerless lives, make up for it as much as they can by owning powerful machines. The more menial your job, the greater your desire to spend your spare time scaring the wits out of people with your huge motorcycle. Or dominating the woods with your snowmobile.

That won't wash, either. *All* classes in America like powerful machinery. People with very unmenial jobs still get excited about Mercedes-Benzes, and like to dominate the fast lanes. The really rich go in for private jets. We need a third principle.

I suspect, though I can't prove it, that the real reason is that both snowmobiling and cross-country skiing started as rural sports. And to the rural mind the key difference is that one is a great deal more work than the other.

A countryman's life consists, basically, of an endless amount of physical activity. You get up early in the morning in order to do the chores: feeding livestock, milking, cleaning the barn, etc. As soon as chores are finished, you go off to fix fence. As soon as that's done, you climb on the tractor and start mowing rowen. Since it's just one of the givens that you are going to be tired every night, you never waste a movement if you can help it. It is for this reason that summer people are sometimes amazed and even scornful to see a native who is cutting wood throw his chainsaw in a truck and drive three hundred yards back into the woods to where he is working. *They* would have walked, carrying the saw, saving gas, observing the beauties of nature. They are environmentalists; he's a clod. Actually, he's just saving a little extra energy for splitting wood.

It is this Principle of Conservation of Energy, I think, that originally determined who rode snowmobiles and who put on the cross-countries. In the old days, rural people simply didn't go out much in the winter—except to bring in wood and do chores. They could have; they had surplus time and energy both. The work of a farm is lightest in the winter. But the principle is deeply ingrained, and their instinctive preference was to hang around the house, being bored if necessary, rather than go out and do a lot of hard slogging through the snow in pursuit of something as ephemeral as mere pleasure. It is for the same reason that Midwestern grain farmers, who are richer and don't have chores, tend to go to Florida in the winter. Florida is essentially the big house around which they hang, until it's time for spring planting.

Then snowmobiles came along. "Ski-doos" they were first called in New England, after the original Canadian make. Every person in the country perked up his or her head. I stress "her" because ski-doos were especially appealing to rural wives. All spring, summer, and fall they were used to working as hard in the house (and sometimes the barn, too) as their husbands did out in the fields and woods. With so much cooking to do, lots of them became pretty hefty women.

Now suddenly here was a way to go effortlessly out in the winter—and not only that, you're riding on the same machine with your husband. A second honeymoon! The two of you may revisit, traveling at high speed up the mountainsides, places you once picnicked when you were carefree courting youngsters. I know one elderly farm couple in Vermont, avid snowmobilers, who particularly like to visit his old work sites. Fifty years ago, they were just-married and didn't have a cent. It was in the depth of the great depression. He would be out chopping cordwood for two dollars a cord. She would walk all the way out to where he was, to bring him his dinner (which is what country people eat for lunch) in a pail. Now they whoosh out by snowmobile and recall old times.

But, of course, rural people are not the only ones who live in the country. There are also large numbers of urbanites. There are the summer people, the young college graduates who have joined the counter-culture and moved here for good, the people with year-round second homes. Their working lives have been very different—mostly cooped up in offices. If they're tired at night, it's from too much mental tension. Their bodies cry out for use. So their principle has been that when you have free time, you try to find a way to use up energy as rapidly as possible. (This is the true and original cause of jogging.)

Consequently, they tend to see the countryside as a sort of enormous gymnasium, just as Midwestern farmers see Florida as an enormous living room. They naturally opt for skis. And their Principle of Hard Play, like the countryman's conservation of energy principle, applies even when the original conditions don't. The young back-to-the-landers aren't cooped up in offices; they're out logging with horses, or spading up a two-acre garden. But come the first big snow, they wouldn't dream of going out on a machine. Childhood conditioning is too strong. They snap on their skis, load a little backpack with gorp, and go out to spend even more energy.

I have been in an especially good position to observe all

this, because I happen to be right in the middle. I am one of perhaps ten people in my part of Vermont who is both a snowmobiler and a cross-country skier. I really like both sports. This reflects a deep division in my whole life. Half the time I am a middle-class teacher at Dartmouth, and the other half I am a working-class farmer. I mow fields on contract to summer people, sell wood and stack it for the customers, know what it's like to be one of the help. ("That's not where I told you to stack it," the lady informs me in a cool, regal voice; "move the pile behind the garage.") I am so deeply into rurality that my own childhood conditioning has almost been overcome.

There's just enough left, though, so that I understand very well why cross-country skiers despise snowmobilers. Sometimes when I'm out on skis I do myself. Yes, snow machines are noisy. Smelly, too—fouling the crisp winter air with their exhausts. Yes, it's annoying to spend two hours skiing to some remote and peaceful ridge, alone or with a silent friend, and to think you are utterly away from everything—and suddenly a herd of nine snowmobilers roars up right behind you, and thunders on over the ridge, all but throwing beer cans at you as they pass. Maybe damaging the young forest growth without either knowing or caring. And, yes, it can just about wreck a weekend if some neighbor's nine-year-old child spends most of the daylight hours on daddy's machine, going monotonously round and round one field, wasting gas, forever gunning the engine, doing something very close to profaning the Sabbath. In such moods I reflect quite gleefully that as fuel prices continue to rise, snow machines may just up and vanish. At least in New England, they are already in decline. Ten years ago, there were 26,654 registered in Vermont. Five years ago, still building: there were 34,715. Now the number has shrunk to 22,107.

But when it's my own daughter out circling our own back pasture, I feel quite differently. Then I admire the skill with which she takes sharp turns on a steep hillside, and the daring of her jumps. I love to see her shining eyes as she comes in from the kind of morning she wouldn't dream of spending on skis.

And when I go out myself, which is usually with a few farmer friends and mechanics, there are two things I understand. One is the sheer pleasure of hurtling headlong across the landscape, and winding up in places one might otherwise never have reached in a lifetime. A clifftop two towns away, say, known to no one but the snowmobilers and an occasional hawk or owl. The damned skiers think we don't notice nature, because we're too busy steering our machines. What they don't realize is that we're usually going somewhere—a further place than *they're* likely to get —and when we reach it, we stop and dismount. Then we see everything. Especially the good views, since we go up a lot of hills. We know their landscape better than they do, as a rule. (A lot of skiers just shuffle around golf courses, anyway—jogging with flaps on their feet.)

The other thing I understand is just how infuriating the middle class is, with its assumptions of moral superiority. They used to say we kept coal in our bathtubs. (If you have a stove right near the bathroom, it can be a handy place, too.) Then they criticized us for having big TV sets when we were poor, and buying expensive cars on time. They didn't stop to reflect that if we didn't buy on time, they wouldn't be *getting* fourteen percent on their money. They need our installment payments to run their economy.

And now they scorn us for our snow machines. They're the ones who are aggressive, not us. If any of them are up here in the winter, they'll call the police in a minute if we go across a corner of "their" land. Even if, and perhaps especially if, it was land they bought from one of us about two years ago. They're the ones who pointedly avert their faces when we pass—do all but hold their noses. We're willing to share the outdoors with them, but they'd like to abolish us. (Though the ones that dare to venture off the golf courses and their little pre-arranged routes seem surprisingly often to take advantage of the trails we've packed down. Then they're outraged if one of us happens to come along our own trail that we made, while they're using it. They think they own that, too.)

I know what they say. They say we are perfectly welcome to be outdoors, but we should all learn to cross-country ski ourselves. Including Aunt Etty, who is sixty-eight, weighs 185, and has varicose veins. Maybe it would be better for Aunt Etty if she were only thirty-eight, weighed 125, and skied like an angel. But she's not an angel, she's a fat old lady who still works hard (she cleaned your house last week, skier), and this is the only way she'll ever be out here, and she loves it.

And you, you want to take her snow machine away, because it spoils your image of rural New England. It offends your eardrums. But you're smart, skier. You don't say that. You say in a sincere voice that she'd really be far happier, and in much better health, if she did high-energy sports like you.

One time one of you told us to eat cake, and that advice was just about as useful.

Farm Flowers

I ONCE SAW A BEAUTIFUL SWISS POSTER, part of a campaign to save wildflowers. In neat ranks of five, it showed color photographs of twenty-five protected varieties that grow in the Alps: edelweiss, the white St. Bruno's lily, yellow houseleek, aquilegia alpina, and so forth.

At the bottom were four captions. And here was where the poster became delightful, funny—and something of a key to national temperaments as the Swiss perceive them. Each caption was in a different language. Each language made a different appeal.

First came the German, slightly gruff and stressing decency. "Protect our plants," it began. (Well, being in German, it actually began *Schützt unser Pflanzen.*) "Good manners and the law forbid picking or digging them up," it concluded. One can easily imagine a German couple standing in front of a patch of houseleek, itching to pick a few, but restraining themselves when they reflect that to do so would not only be illegal but also rude.

Then came the French version, much more flowery (so to speak) and emotional. "Let us conserve these treasures for our children!" it somewhat shrilly urged. Conserve these treasures? To my ear, at least, there's a hint of French avarice here: the gold safely hidden in the mattress, the wildflowers safely hidden on the hill. The French reader is then told why the wildflowers must stay on the hill. "The law and our conscience forbid us to pick them or to dig them up." Conscience is personal, as opposed to good manners, which is a group characteristic. If the poster is right, Gallic culture is inner-directed; Teutonic, other-directed.

And, alas, if the poster is right, Mediterranean culture is snobbish. "No educated person will either pick or eradicate these plants," the Italian caption elegantly states. "Also, the law forbids it."

In other words, to be seen with a St. Bruno's lily in your hand marks you as a peasant. You may not have any manners, and you may lack a conscience, not to mention respect for the law, but having been to *seminario*, or being *laureato*, you are bound to leave the flowers alone.

Finally, there was the English caption: flat and matter-of-fact, sounding almost like an EPA regulation. "It is forbidden by law to pick or dig up the listed plants." Apparently Englishmen and Americans have *no* interesting characteristics; we merely process information.

But there is obviously one thing the four captions have in common. They take it for granted that wildflowers are sacrosanct. Whether it's a matter of saving treasures for the future or observing human decency or showing one's status doesn't matter, it all comes to the same thing. One doesn't pick aquilegia.

I am going to argue that to think this way is to diminish wildflowers, by treating them as more fragile than they are. If they are *never* to be picked, and never to be dug up, then they are museum pieces, and they will suffer the same loss of reality that Old Master paintings have. (When the last Rembrandt is out of private hands and into a museum, then Rembrandt will be totally dead, as all treasure is dead. It's there to be admired and catalogued and guarded by dragons, but change and growth have ceased.)

Of course I think there should be laws protecting endangered species, and of course I am aware that there are people who make a business of systematically digging up and selling rare wildflowers, and I am delighted when one of them is caught and punished. I am even aware that the more human beings there are (and we've added the last billion in exactly twelve years), the greater need there is to protect the environment from our grabby hands and acquisitive instincts.

All the same, it is possible to be overzealous in this matter of protection. Wildflowers are not even nearly so helpless as myth would sometimes have it. At least, they're not where I live.

Where I live is on a farm with roughly thirty-two acres of pasture and one hundred fifty acres of woods. Nothing is ever plowed (except a small vegetable garden), and both the pastures and the woods are full of wildflowers. The field flowers of course are the common ones: ranging from the golden river of dandelions that flows down the back pasture each spring to the usual scattering of buttercups and black-eyed Susans and Quaker ladies. In the woods, and especially in the fringe-land between trees and field, we have some moderately rarer ones: columbine, ladies'-tresses, red trillium and showy orchis.

The field flowers lead lives of constant danger, since the fields are full of cattle. Cattle know nothing about conserving treasures. The cows step on the flowers, eat them (they won't touch buttercups, but they seem to like violets just fine), casually dump cow-flops on them, sometimes lie down and spend the night on a whole bed of them. All these assaults seem, if anything, to be invigorating. The field flowers thrive.

But it's the allegedly fragile woods flowers that are at issue. Columbine, for example. Columbine is not actually a protected plant in Vermont, like its aquilegia cousins in Switzerland, but it's no common daisy, either. Columbine gets respect.

I know about patches of columbine in at least three different places around this farm. One patch, at the base of a low cliff, has a hundred or so plants scattered here and there. And about ten years ago, my educated, conscientious, well-mannered wife decided that it would be perfectly moral to dig a couple of them up and move them to our front yard. She did. And not to some shady nook among the periwinkle, either, which would partially replicate wild conditions, but to an actual flower border in front of the house. Guess what's happened since. There are about a dozen columbines in that border now, blooming like crazy, and new ones often pop up out in the lawn. If we ever quit cutting the grass, we'd have a columbine nursery.

Similarly with trillium. At least on my farm, it doesn't grow in patches, but as isolated plants distributed through maybe a quarter of the woods. A few years ago we dug up just one plant, and this we did put in a shady corner by a stone wall. It's still there. And whether it has been busy propagating ever since, or whether it's just that I've been noticing trillium more since the guilty deed, I have to report that we have trillium the way some people have tulips.

There are four or five growing along the hay lane. Half a dozen on the shady north side of the little sheep pasture just above the house. (The sheep are profoundly indifferent to them, being picky eaters and also quite blind to aesthetics.) There's even one that keeps stubbornly growing out from under the woodpile.

I have never moved a showy orchis, and don't plan to. I don't strike children, either. But I will claim to be on better terms with the flora of this farm—loving, using, and occasionally abusing it—than if I spent all my time tiptoeing reverently around and putting up little signs. Preservation is good, but normal life is better.

Low Technology in the Sugarbush

ONE DAY AROUND THE MIDDLE of March it begins.
There's been a good frost the night before, and today is
warm and sunny. Not much wind. Maple sap, which has
been dripping very slowly from spouts for a few days now,
starts to drip fast. On the south sides of the best trees, it
might even run in a tiny trickle. A new sugar season has
begun.

In Vermont that means two very different kinds of operation get under way. Both wind up with the same products: cans of maple syrup, jars of maple sugar, boxes of
maple candy. Both are a contradiction of the usual laws of
farming, which say that you plant a crop in the spring,
tend it in the summer, and harvest it in the fall. For two
hundred years Vermonters have harvested their first cash
crop even before spring has come, even before the earliest
farmer in the southernmost county in Mississippi has a
thing to sell. It may well be the one agricultural advantage
Vermont has.

The two kinds of operation are, of course, high-technology and low-technology sugaring. They are about as different as a textile factory and a girl with a spinning wheel.

That both can thrive in the same state at the same time is a kind of miracle.

Twenty years ago it looked as though high-technology sugaring would take over completely. Why not? High technology generally does win. It may be less picturesque, but it's cheaper. Take the little flocks of hens that farmers' wives used to keep. They were charming. They still are, in the pictures in children's books. But in the real world they have been almost totally replaced by large, ugly, efficient battery houses, where maybe fifty thousand hens are jammed in together, and constitute a kind of living factory. No roosters, no chicks to peep and run about, no soil to peck. Just an assembly line for eggs. But even more economical than it is cruel. In one generation, a few hundred battery houses replaced a hundred thousand farmers' wives.

In the sugaring world, things seemed to be headed the same way. High technology duly arrived, with polyvinyl plastic in one hand and a stack of motors in the other. By all logic, the result should have been a wave of consolidations, and finally a few giant producers taking over the whole maple industry. But that hasn't happened. On the contrary, there are more people making maple syrup now than there have been for half a century. Most of them are small producers, using old-fashioned methods. It's an encouraging story.

In the beginning (and still sometimes in popular memory), sugaring was done with wooden buckets that you hung on the trees, and big iron kettles that you made the syrup in. There's such a kettle in the cellar of my house. It's thirty-two inches in diameter and weighs a hundred pounds.

After the Civil War, technology moved up a notch. By 1875 farmers hung metal buckets from their trees, and they made the syrup in evaporators which boiled maybe ten times faster than the old iron kettles. But neither of these changes made the operation less picturesque. Farm families still emptied the buckets by hand. They still hitched a team of horses to a sled when it came time to gather. And they still did the boiling over huge wood fires.

But to do all that is a very great deal of work. Say you were a farmer with a real sugarbush—that is, a large stand of hard maples bunched close together but not too close, which you trimmed and tended regularly. Say your aim was to make five or six hundred gallons of syrup each spring.

To do that, you had to go out with a hand drill and bore about twenty-five hundred tap-holes in your trees. (The rule of thumb was and still is that you can make a quart of syrup per tap in a good year.) Then you had to drive in twenty-five hundred spouts. Then hang twenty-five hundred buckets on those spouts. Then fit a specially designed lid on each, to keep the snow out.

So far, all you had done was to get ready. Once the sap started to run, serious work began. You had to go around every day or two and empty all those buckets. In the right kind of weather, they'd average a gallon of sap each, or better. So you then had to haul three or four thousand gallons of sap over to your sugarhouse. Ten or twelve tons of sloshing sap. Then you could start boiling. When you were done, many hours later, you had your first seventy-five or one hundred gallons of syrup—which you still had to put in cans. By then it was time to go gather again.

So when high technology came along, in the form of

eager plastics manufacturers, there were a lot of interested producers. The new system worked like this. Now you went out with a gasoline-powered tapping drill hung around your neck. Noisy but fast. Having drilled all your holes, you linked them up with slender plastic pipe, a pale lavender kind originally developed for use in hospitals. These little pipes fed into bigger ones, and eventually a main line went right to the sugarhouse. Of course, unless your maple grove happened to be on a hillside, the sap wasn't going to flow in by itself. The system took account of that. You installed a powerful vacuum pump in the sugarhouse, and sucked the sap right out of the trees. There was some evidence you could get a little more than they really wanted to give.

You still had to do your boiling with an evaporator. (On the scale we're talking about, you'd probably use two of them in parallel, each four feet wide by fourteen feet long.) But instead of stoking it with maple trimmings, plus all the junk wood you'd gathered up around your farm, plus slabs from the nearest sawmill, you flicked a switch and your oil burner roared into life. Meanwhile, goodby to the buckets and horses and leaping fires.

Two things intervened to save traditional sugaring. One was the dramatic rise in the price of oil. Where in 1970 it took about sixty cents' worth of oil to make a gallon of maple syrup, now it takes around four dollars' worth— three gallons of oil for each gallon of syrup. The waste of fossil fuel isn't necessarily a deterrent, but the four dollars is. The big manufacturers of sugaring equipment (there are three of them, two in Vermont and one in Canada) still make oil-fired equipment, but they're not selling a whole lot of it. There has been a major shift back to wood.

The other thing is the nature of maple trees themselves. They are not a bit portable. Neither do they grow fast. Forty years is a good average from the time you plant a sugar maple until the time you can start tapping it. So while it may be easy to herd a lot of chickens into a rural ghetto, lock them in cages for life, and automate egg production, nobody is going to herd a lot of maples anywhere. You have to take them where you find them. And lots of them are to be found in small clumps, or in a row of a dozen huge old trees in front of a farmhouse, or even scattered one by one around a farm.

For maples like these, pipeline and vacuum pumps are not practical. Buckets are actually easier. And since we're now talking about relatively small numbers, not a big sugarbush, things like power tapping drills and steam hoods and reverse osmosis are just so many unnecessary expenses. A person who is making only two or three hundred taps finds the old ways remarkably efficient. Such a producer can make his or her sixty or eighty gallons of syrup a year, sell it at the same price as the big fellows, and make the same margin of profit or better. There are hundreds and hundreds of such producers all over New England—and some in New York and Pennsylvania, too. And there are thousands more who run still smaller operations: maybe thirty taps, maybe one hundred and twenty-five. I'm one of them myself. Down here on Level Three, the equipment can be very primitive indeed. Much of it is apt to be homemade. But we, too, can sell syrup in competition with the man that has five thousand taps on pipeline. We're the exact equivalent of those farmers' wives making pin money with their little flocks of hens. Only, we still exist.

How does a small sugar operation work? Well, practically every one is different. We all have containers hanging on maple trees, and we all have some way of boiling down the sap. The rest varies. For example, I myself hang a hundred old buckets that I bought at a mountain auction in 1962, and that were probably fifty years old then. Most of my trees are along roadsides, and I gather the sap by truck. Boil it down in a small but very professional evaporator made by Grimm & Co. in Rutland. My average production is twenty-seven gallons a year, and I sell most of it by mail to out-of-staters. The rest goes on our own table.

One of my neighbors, a young wife and mother, has all spanking new buckets with shiny lids, about thirty of them. She gathers on foot, sometimes using an old sap yoke such as they used two hundred years ago. She does her boiling in a flat pan set up on concrete blocks just outside her kitchen—and dashes out about once every half hour to tend the fire. Her rate of production is very little faster than it was for the pre-Civil-War farmers. But she still makes her seven gallons a year. Most of that she puts in fancy little cans to use as Christmas presents. And each spring, between the gathering and the dashes, she gets a good deal of exercise that she professes to find more interesting than jogging.

Another nearby producer is a teenage boy. He uses around fifty one-gallon plastic milk cartons to hang on his trees. A true sap bucket holds either four or five gallons (there are two sizes), so that on the rare days you get really good sap runs, the buckets don't spill over. If there's an exceptional run on a day when Tim's at high school, either he loses sap or his mother has to gather for him. But, of course, his "buckets" cost him nothing. For boiling he has a homemade evaporator, made from a fifty-five-gallon drum. One of his uncles is a pretty good welder, and made it up for him for Christmas. Tim produces a dozen gallons a year.

Still another is a chaired professor at Dartmouth, a man nearing sixty. He has exactly seven trees in a mini-grove by his garage. Those seven are legendary for starting to run sooner than anyone else's, though, and for producing remarkable volumes of sap. Some people think there is a mystic connection between the surging oratory of Jim's lectures and the copious flow of his trees. In fact, violating the whole rational side of my nature, I think it, too. Jim makes exactly what they consume on the place: about three gallons a year.

Then there's my friend Alice, who lives one town away. Her trees are in a big hillside grove, far from any road. She and her husband couldn't gather by truck even if they wanted to, which they don't. They do it with a team of Belgian workhorses, pulling a heavy wooden sledge.

Alice loves hanging buckets (hers are even older than mine), and sometimes puts up a couple of hundred. Then, because three small children take a lot of time, and also because a team of Belgians is hard for a woman who probably doesn't weigh much over a hundred pounds to harness by herself, she has trouble keeping them emptied. Her production varies wildly. In a year when her husband can get off work enough to help her, it might be fifty gallons; another year it might be barely twenty. What runs high every year is the number of children who get a ride through the snowy woods on her sledge.

Sugaring is not one kind of activity, but many. I have no objection to the pipeline variety—I've even tried it myself —so long as it doesn't wipe out the bucket and coffee-can varieties. Because the loss would be huge.

Low Technology in the Sugarbush

Low technology is more than a sentimental pleasure—though God knows it's that. It is a kind of salvation for people. We live in a time when most of us, in our work, are servants of machines (and a handful, of course, are masters). In terms of the gross national product, that has worked out very nicely. In terms of the process of daily living, it has been a good deal less satisfactory. The more things there can be like sugaring, where simple and easily understood techniques can compete in the marketplace with automation, the more sense of ourselves as valuable and needed beings we will be able to keep. And that's a sense every human being and even every chicken ought to have.

How to Farm Badly
(and Why You Should)

IN ONE OF ALBERT PAYSON TERHUNE'S dog books, there is a background figure of a rich city man who has bought a farm. His first act is to stock it with prize cattle and pedigreed sheep. Then he buys a lot of expensive farm machinery. Finally, eyes shining, he sets out to improve the pastures (he wants to grow prize hay), build the best fences in the county, and in general turn his farm into a showplace.

Terhune wrote that account sixty years ago. But the tendency he describes is still very much in evidence. When city people buy an old farm, not just as a venue for lawn parties, but because they are converts to country life, they usually get carried away. They start to fix up the whole farm the way you might fix up the interior of an old house.

This impulse is highly understandable. I have a bad case of Improver's Itch myself. A month seldom goes by that I don't fix up something or other on my own farm, even if it's only rebuilding a couple of rods of stone wall. Over the years I've handled a surprising amount of stone that serves no farm purpose whatsoever, and hasn't since wire fencing came in. But I love doing it.

Furthermore, in the case of people who have bought a

run-down old place, the impulse to fix is not only under-standable but necessary. There are apt to be dead cars behind the barn. It makes every kind of sense to get them quickly off to a junk dealer. The fields are likely to be growing up to brush. The faster you start clearing, the better. Old fruit trees are sure to need pruning. The day you move in is not too soon to start—provided you know how to prune. All that I concede.

But the minute anyone starts thinking "showplace," he or she is inviting about six kinds of trouble. Unless like Terhune's Wall Street Farmer, you *want* to sink an annual fortune into the place—and unless like him you have a crew of hired hands to solve all the problems you are certain to create—you will be well advised to start out farming badly.

That statement needs immediate clarification. There is one kind of bad farming that is pure laziness or sheer igno-rance, and that is a matter of not taking the one stitch now that will save nine later. In no way am I recommending it. Then there is a second kind that is bad farming only by the standards of agribusiness. What it requires is accepting your own limits and the limits of your land, and having the sense not to try for results that exceed those limits. This is what I am talking about.

Let me be as clear as possible. I don't mean letting a hillside field erode into gullies because you plowed it wrong. Certainly I don't mean getting a little flock of sheep and then watching them die of intestinal parasites because you didn't know about boluses and balling guns. I don't mean *anything* that harms the land.

What I do mean is avoiding most high technology. Not trying to achieve the "best" anything. Ignoring most (not all) advice put out by the U.S. Department of Agriculture. Or to put it positively, being content with moderate yields, modest improvements, slow changes, old equipment. Being content with this for the first five years, anyway, and probably even after that, unless you've meanwhile turned into a professional farmer. (In which case you may not be reading books like this, anyway, which you'll regard as sentimental. You'll be reading *Hog Farm Management* or *Agrichemical Age*.)

Enough of exhortation, though. Examples are what convince. Let me give some. They'll be Horrible Examples, of people who did try for the best, that person most usually being myself. Let me start with sheep.

Sheep have made a comeback in America since 1970. It is increasingly common for city people with country places to buy a few as their first venture into farming. Most do a little preliminary research—and quickly discover that they have a complicated choice to make. That's true with anything one looks at closely. When I was a boy in the suburbs, I thought there were three kinds of potatoes—or would have if I had ever bothered to concentrate on so boring a subject. I thought there were real potatoes, sweet potatoes, and something called an Idaho potato, which you baked. Since I've been a farmer, I've personally grown fifteen varieties of potato, including the purplish ones shaped like and called Cow Horns, and am aware there are hundreds of others.

So in the ovine world. The newcomer finds that there is not just one woolly animal called "sheep," as in the cute kids' ads, but instead breed after breed. Nearly all sound appealing: tall lordly Suffolks with their dark faces and rapid weight gains, Romneys that yield such tasty legs of lamb, Finn crosses that are so incredibly prolific. The newcomer sits around ticking off the advantages of each and wondering which to get, as one might compare gas mileage, comfort, and acceleration when buying a car.

The one thing the newcomer doesn't consider, usually, is getting an unpedigreed sheep. True, they're cheaper. (Last year a friend of mine got a sort of mongrel ewe at an auction for $22—and within a week she had twin lambs, which makes three sheep at $7.33 each. But that was an exceptional case.) The difference isn't likely to be huge. You can usually get a good pedigreed lamb for sixty or seventy dollars, where you might pay thirty or forty dollars for a common animal. To a middle-class American, used to shelling out two or three thousand extra for a car that pleases him, what's thirty bucks? Go for the good stuff, he thinks.

Certainly it's what I thought when I got my first two lambs, which were Dorsets. What I failed to reflect on was that nearly all pedigreed sheep are highly specialized creatures. They've been bred for maximum wool yield, or maximum meat yield, or maximum breeding speed. They've had that done to them for hundreds of generations. What human beings have cheerfully sacrificed on their behalf is versatility and resilience. All sheep die easily, but on the whole pedigreed sheep have an even feebler grasp on life than ordinary sheep. They're also more likely to need assistance in birthing. Owners of high-class sheep are often in the barn at 3:00 A.M. on a cold March night, helping to deliver high-class twins.

Neither of these, though, is the reason I wish now I had started with a couple of common lambs. My reason is grazing habits.

I had several aims in mind when I bought lambs. One, of course, was fresh lamb chops, organically raised. Another was sheepskins to put on car seats—it really does keep them cool—and daughters' beds. But my main motive was to acquire a mobile weed-trimming unit. I had a small orchard that I wanted to clear of weeds and brush without getting into plowing and reseeding. I imagined my two little Dorset ram lambs tirelessly chewing away at the hard-hack and goldenrod.

They did, I admit, eat the poison ivy patch that had come into one corner of the orchard. And sometimes they would nibble daintily at young dandelions. Otherwise, they ate only grass, and only certain kinds of that, and only at certain early growth stages. I'm not blaming them. They had been bred to put on weight fast; and to do it at the rate they were genetically conditioned for, they needed the best high-protein grass. Plus grain on the side.

Low-bred sheep, on the other hand, are used to making do with what's available. They have their preferences, to be sure, but lacking first, second, and third choice, they can keep hide and hoofs together on almost any kind of pasture. They're what in New England used to be called thrifty keepers. They're what I should have bought. I might not have had any papers to show, but I would have gotten my orchard cleared. (Especially if I'd bought half a dozen lambs, instead of two.)

Time for another example. Following the Wall Street Farmer, let's turn now to land improvement. Almost any-one buying an old farm is likely to get a worn-out field or two with the place. The grass is thin; there are ferns com-ing in; whole patches are spotted with moss. Sure signs of acidity and poor soil.

There is a natural and healthy tendency to want to re-store such fields to good condition: have some soil tests made, order the lime and fertilizer, maybe get some clover and vetch going. I'm for it. So is everybody else. The county agent may be able to show you how you can get the government to help pay for the lime. Any agricultural text, old or new, is full of instructions to fertilize. Even poetry points that way.

> *What is more accursed*
> *Than an impoverished soil, pale and metallic?*
> *What cries more to our kind for sympathy?*

says Robert Frost in the poem "Build Soil." Horace and Vergil held the same view.

So, fine. Lime and fertilize. Spread manure, if you have any. But if you take my advice, you'll do all these things in moderation. Try for good grass, but not exceptional grass —because if you have exceptional grass, it's going to require exceptional care. Again, an example from my own experience.

Behind my house there is a fairly good hayfield. Seven acres. It has only a few stones and no slopes too steep to mow. With a little lime every decade and a little manure every year, it consistently yields 250 to 300 bales of hay a year. I mow it, and a neighbor with more equipment comes and does the raking and baling for me. We need only two sunny days. If I start mowing on Tuesday morning as soon as the dew is off, he can rake on Wednesday afternoon and bale before supper. That night the hay is safely in the barn, and it's nice bright dry hay. Then we let the grass recover for two or three weeks and turn calves in for the rest of the summer.

A decent seven-acre field *can*, of course, yield much more than 250 to 300 bales. Even in a single cutting, it can be made to yield twice that. Once a few years ago, when I had some horses to winter as well as my usual two or three beef cattle, I decided it would be silly to buy the extra hay when I could just as easily have a prize field. So I loaded it with chemical fertilizer.

The results were apparent right away. Grass that had been ten inches high the year before went up to twenty; and in the swales where it had been high to begin with, it looked something like a bamboo grove.

You can see what's coming. That year I harvested the smallest quantity of good hay I have ever gotten. The mowing went all right, though slower than usual because the swathes were so heavy, and I kept bunching it up at the turns. But after that I had a steady series of disasters. I knew that heavy hay would be hard to dry, and I had been able to borrow a hay conditioner (an old one that worked something like a laundry wringer). In the intervals between getting the conditioner jammed, I was able to wring the juice out of most of the really tall grass. That helped—or at least I'm determined to think it did—but it didn't help enough.

When my friend came to rake, he took one pitying look, and went home and got his tedder. In case you're not familiar with tedders, they're spidery-looking devices that turn thick grass over so that the sun can get at the bottom side. Then he waited a day and came back and raked. Some swathes were fully dry, and some weren't. On that third afternoon, the sun still holding, we baled about ninety bales of good hay—and about thirty more with green locks, that would probably go musty. The rest we left. I spent until dark with a pitchfork, fluffing up the windrows. What I accomplished was to enable the nice rain we had the next morning to soak in even better.

Eventually we did get it all baled, and there was a lot.

Nearly five hundred bales. Of course I figure it cost me about two-fifty a bale for rained-on hay in a year when one could easily buy bright hay for one-fifty a bale. I had been trying to farm too well.

You can say that's just me. A competent farmer (with lots of equipment) would have managed better. So he would have. But, then, few newcomers *are* competent farmers in the first few years. Besides, I have more examples that are not personal.

A friend of mine—pretty good farmer, too—has a sideline of making cider. The farm he inherited had about a hundred old apple trees, most of them not worth saving, he decided. So he pulled out about seventy of them and planted new classy stock from a nursery. Most of them died, being specialized, delicate, high-yield creatures, much like pedigreed sheep, and beyond his skill to care for. Meanwhile, the thirty surviving oldsters, helped by a good pruning, went right on yielding quite a lot of apples. They weren't big, and they weren't beautiful, but they made wonderful cider. Not so with the culls he was getting from a nearby big and beautiful orchard while waiting for his trees to grow. He got a lot of juice out of them, but not much flavor. If he could resurrect the seventy tough old trees, he'd do it.

Well, maybe he wasn't smart, either, so here's another example, one that doesn't involve anyone I know. This is just about a dairy farmer I've heard of, who upgraded his herd of milkers.

Most dairy farmers in America now keep Holsteins. There are still Jerseys and Guernseys and milking short-horns around, but Holsteins are the norm, for the simple reason that they are enormous cows with enormous udders that give enormous amounts of milk. There is, however, a price to pay for all this enormousness, and I don't just mean their enormous appetites.

Anyone who has seen a Holstein milker (many people haven't, because once grown, Holsteins are often confined in a barn for life)—any such person knows that here is an animal that has been bred into distortion. A Holstein cow is basically a support system for an udder. So much so that the biggest and "best" Holsteins walk rather the way camp followers used to when they were smuggling whisky to the troops during the Civil War. Which is how? Well, those were the days when dresses reached the ground. Men, even military police, knew it was highly improper to lift anyone's skirt. So the camp follower would put a pair of suspenders on under her dress—and from them she would suspend a five-gallon can of whisky, which hung between her legs. Naturally this gave her a somewhat waddling walk. That's more or less how Holstein cows look, once they have made bag.

An udder that big is, of course, in a constant state of tension. Most Holsteins are perpetually on the verge of getting mastitis, alias inflammation of the breast, which is one reason there are antibiotics in most cattle feed. Some of them have to wear a sort of horrible parody of a bra called a Tamm udder support. It fastens with a lot of straps across the cow's back. You can get your cow one for about fifty-five dollars.

The farmer I read about already had Holsteins. He just wanted ones with extra-big udders, which would yield an extra thousand or two pounds of milk a year. So he did a bit of genetic engineering. That is, he bought semen from a bull whose get were guaranteed to be even more distorted than most Holsteins.

Result: his next crop of heifers looked as if they were

carrying *six* gallons of whisky between their legs. Or maybe eight. Too much, anyway, for flesh to take the strain. The result was the bovine equivalent of a hernia. It's called a prolapsed udder, and what happens is that the udder droops until it drags on the ground. Not all his new heifers had their udders tear loose—if I remember correctly, it was no more than one in four or five. But it was enough so that he'd have been further ahead if he'd farmed a little worse. Further ahead economically, I mean. With heroic restraint, I'm not even raising any of the moral questions I see involved here.

Well, it's human to make mistakes, and maybe that was just a dumb dairy farmer I read about. So for my last example, I'm going to use a case that doesn't involve people at all. It involves forage.

Corn, hay, and oats are the classic forage crops in this country, but there are many, many others. Millet, for example, and mangel-wurzels, the giant beets that figure as a comic effect in the novels of P. G. Wodehouse. In the last generation, sudan grass and several kinds of sorghum have become increasingly popular forages with American farmers. They're often served as a kind of salad (the technical name is green-chop) to animals that aren't allowed out in the fields—milking Holsteins, say, or beef cattle in that special western hell known as the feedlot.

Guess what. If you grow sudan grass or sorghum and are content with a reasonable yield, you can give it freely to cattle. But if you really put the fertilizer to it, you will poison the cows. What happens is that the prussic acid always present in sudan grass and sorghum shoots up to toxic levels the minute you try for maximum production.

I think sudan grass and sorghum are trying to tell us something.

The Beef Cow's Plea to the Vegetarians

MICHEL DU BOS
% NOEL PERRIN
THETFORD CTR., VT.

DEAR VEGETARIANS,

Allow me first to introduce myself. My name is Michel. I am a two-year-old Hereford steer living in Vermont. "Michel" is, of course, what my owners call me; in the herd we don't use names. We go mostly by smell, and a little by sight. There is no way I can reproduce my scent-name in human speech.

While I'm at it, there is one other thing to confess. I obviously don't think in human patterns (though I do think, and in more complex ways than most people realize). One consequence of *that* is that I can neither read nor write. I have had considerable help with this article from a human collaborator.

Now let me get right to my plea. I wish you vegetarians would not work so hard trying to discourage people from eating meat. Because if you succeed, I and my kind will cease to exist. Oh, I suppose zoos will keep a few of us—but where there are millions of us Herefords and our Angus and Charolais cousins in the United States now, if people were to quit eating beef, there would soon be fewer of us than there are buffalo. A few thousand, maybe.

At least I wish you would stop doing it on the grounds that it is somehow wrong to eat meat. If you simply don't like the taste of beef, that's quite another matter. As a vegetarian myself, I can understand that perfectly. It's your moral crusade that bothers me. I don't want to be extinct. And if I must be, I want to be sure you understand exactly what you are doing.

You will retort that you have no plans to kill me: it's my owner who intends to do that. And of course you are right. He does. This year. But meanwhile I have had a good and an interesting life, and it's that I want to tell you about first. I have another thing to say afterwards.

I was born here on this farm in long-grass time two years ago. Apart from flies, my first three months were pure bliss. We cattle have the best part of the farm: two big connected pastures, with sunny spots and cool spots; a nice wallow; a hill that we usually climb on hot nights, because there's always a breeze on top. We have two different groves of trees for when it's stormy, and a shed my owner built besides. We never use the shed except in winter, and not too much then. It's more fun to be out.

Cattle are fast developers, and I could outrun any human being by the time I was two days old. At a week I was playing with the two other calves we had in the pasture that year. By the end of a month I had learned how good clover tastes, though of course I lived mainly on milk.

This may be the moment to deal with one argument I understand some of you use against beef cattle. You say it is wrong to feed three or four pounds of grain to a steer like me, so that I can gain one pound, when that grain could be used to feed starving human beings. Naturally I see that you would put your kind first, and I realize it's human beings, not cattle, who grow the grain.

The way some cattle are raised, you certainly have a point, but you don't with me. Our herd lives on grass all summer, and on hay all winter, with maybe one sack of grain per year for every three of us. And if you think our owner could get rid of us and start growing grain in what is now our pasture, then you don't understand much about farming. Most of the pasture is steep. Nearly all of it has rocks. And the whole thing is what's called Class II soil (which is really Class III, because the top class is called Prime). That means it would yield a pathetic grain crop. The real choices are grass or trees. I don't believe you people can eat either.

It's true that the field where my owner cuts our hay is level enough so that you could plow most of it without too much erosion, and it's almost rock-free. But that's Class II soil as well. There's no way he could raise grain there at competitive prices. So don't tell me I'm taking food out of the mouths of starving Third Worlders. I'm not.

When I was three months old, I had my first bad experience. My owner enticed my mother and me and two or three others into a sort of pen he has in the front of the pasture. And then—I'm not going to mince words—a neighbor of his castrated me. The actual pain was quite brief. I don't suppose it's much worse than the circumcision a lot of your males have to endure. But naturally I would far rather have grown up to be a bull. Sex isn't the time-consumer with us it is with you. I've seen a bull—an uncle of mine, in fact—at work, and the whole thing takes maybe twenty seconds. But make no mistake, we enjoy it. I consider my gelding a major deprivation, and I still resent it.

On the other hand, we Herefords are famously an easy-going lot, and that morning in the pen certainly didn't wreck my life. Not only do I have the pleasures of the pasture (there are twenty-seven grasses and legumes that I can rank in order of preference, and that's not counting tree-leaves, which are also delicious); and not only do I have the pleasure of the cud, I am still very much a male, and the heifers know it. I've ridden more than one in my time, and it is quite exciting. And I've had my full share of mutual head-and-neck licking, which I suppose must correspond to cuddling among you people. It's a nice way to spend an hour.

When I was about six months old, the grass stopped growing and the nights began to get long. As I now know, signs of winter. At first it was marvelous. There were no more flies, and the temperature dropped to delightful levels. You people, I understand, evolved in the tropics, and you like it up around seventy. My favorite temperature (except that grass won't grow then) is between twenty and forty Fahrenheit. Not that summer doesn't have its charms —all the seasons do—but a crisp November or December morning is when I feel friskiest. It's the perfect time for a buck and a stamp and a run.

Furthermore, there is considerable pleasure in being

brought one's hay. I don't wait on my owner; he waits on me. He doesn't expect tips, either. I have friends who like hay even in the summer—all of us relish a good bale of bright hay in the winter. Frankly, we live a lot better than our wild ancestors, who were usually half-starved by spring.

The time of deep snow was no special fun, though. Most of the herd had gone home to a neighboring farm. We didn't see them again until spring. There were whole weeks when my mother and I and the two others who stayed in the pasture spent most of our time in the shed. Boring. We had a trail to the watering pond and a trail to the hay feeder, and that was about it. When I tried leaving the trail, the snow came up over my belly.

But we were still a lot better off than the wild deer down the valley. A third of them died that winter. I was never even hungry. I think the truth is that deep winter is a dull time for nearly all the animals in Vermont, including people. It's too dark and too cold. Thirty below feels chilly even to me.

In due course spring came, and I had another wonderful year. From May on, there were eighteen of us in the pasture, all friends. By my first birthday, I was big enough to earn quite a high rank in the herd. When my owner brought us a snack of grain, I always got my share . . . and sometimes a little extra. (If you're thinking hungry Third Worlders, don't. Maybe twice a week he'd provide half a pail for the whole eighteen of us. He just wants to be sure we'll always come when he calls—and we do.)

The next winter was easier, partly because I was almost full-grown and partly because there was less snow. We could and did get around the whole pasture in February.

Even my little half-sister Amanda, who was only seven months old, went everywhere.

Now it's spring again, the clover is up—and I have about six months to live. That part is tough. Of course I don't want to be slaughtered next fall. Of course I'd like to live out the whole twenty-five years of my natural life span. If some rich vegetarian would adopt me as a pet, or if I could pick my own part of India in which to be a sacred cow, I'd jump at it. (India at random doesn't appeal. Too many of those Tharparkar and Red Sindhi cattle have chronic foot-and-mouth disease, and totally inadequate diets as well. You'd think some of them were goats, they're so stunted.)

But—and it's a big but—I would infinitely rather have had these two and a half years than no life at all. Furthermore, I am well aware that I have already lived longer than most of my wild forebears did. The "natural" life span of cattle may be twenty-five years, but in a state of nature damn few of us ever reached it. If I had time-traveled back to be born a baby aurochs or *bos primigenius*, I'd have been lucky to make it to the age of one. More likely some predator would have jumped me when I was a calf, which at least is quick. Or I'd have slowly starved my first winter, as these poor Vermont deer do. A lingering, painful death.

In short, vegetarians, if you can figure out a way to keep me from the slaughterhouse while still guaranteeing me a decent life (and preferably a free one in a pasture, not cramped in some zoo), I'll gladly accept. Otherwise, I'd rather you stayed out of it.

That's not to say there's nothing you can do for us Herefords, because there is. And that leads to my second point. I have had a happy life. Not all beef cattle do. If you want a cause, why not take on the feedlot system, and try to reform it?

Let me tell you about the feedlot system. *That's* where grain gets used lavishly. According to United States Department of Agriculture figures I've seen, something like thirty-five hundred pounds of grain per cow. The system is very common out West, and spreading.

What they do is take a calf away from his mother, ship him to one of these feedlots, and then stuff him full of corn and soybeans, well-sweetened with molasses, until it's time to kill him.

Now personally I have no objection to corn and soybeans. I never met a cow that did. As for molasses, I love the stuff. Not quite as much as I love apples in the fall, but I love it. It's not the diet in a feedlot I object to, not on grounds of taste, anyway, but the life-style. That can best be described as institutionalized cruelty.

Here is a description of a real feedlot, one of two medium-sized ones in a certain county in southwestern Colorado. Partly it's in my words, partly I'm quoting Jeff and Jessica Pearson, a couple of human beings who lived near that lot, and know it well. They wrote a book called *No Time But Place*.

You are to imagine long rows of small pens, each big enough to hold somewhere around a hundred cattle in cramped quarters. There's a concrete "feed bunk" in each pen, which is automatically filled twice a day. There is a water supply. There is also a pervasive stench, night and day, rising from each pen and mingling in the air. (One of the few revenges those cattle get is when the wind blows toward town.) Part of it comes from too much manure and urine tramped under foot. Part of it comes from sick cattle.

The Beef Cow's Plea to the Vegetarians

They're not all sick, but many are, and no wonder. They live in unnatural conditions, jammed in with strangers, eating a diet that's designed not to keep them healthy, but to put flesh on them as fast and as cheaply as possible. Even more of them would be sick if there weren't antibiotics in with the corn.

Here's how the Pearsons describe what it's like for a cow to be sent to Colorado for fattening. I should note that this particular feedlot takes yearling steers and even grown cows, as well as calves from as far away as Florida.

> Weak, exhausted, and emotionally strained from the long overland journey by truck, many of the newcomers develop pneumonia or shipping fever and never recover. . . . Cows and heifers who entered the feedlot pregnant miscarry. The more gluttonous heifers suffer prolapsis: their uteruses pop out and hang, pink and bloody, like large balloons from their hindquarters. Some steers pop their anuses. . . . The dried ground cover of dirt and manure, inhaled, causes respiratory diseases. Abscesses and infections arise from crowding and scraping at the feed bunks and along the pen fences. . . . The alleys are carpeted with the decomposing remains of stillborn calves, some bleached white, others nothing more than black, sunbaked balls of rot.

Now there's a cause for you, vegetarians. Work to outlaw places like that. I don't claim that all feedlots are the living hells that this one is, but all of them are unnatural and unpleasant environments for beef cattle. We were meant for a pastoral life: free to graze and wander.

And if you're wondering why places like that exist, I can give you the answer in one word. Money. Even with the high death-rate, it's a cheap way to fatten us. Cheap because it's automated, and one human being takes care, if you have the nerve to put it that way, of many Herefords. Furthermore, your government encourages it. If you doubt the word of a lowly steer, take a look at Agricultural Economic Report No. 459, published by your government in 1980. "Fattening cattle in feedlots is the cheapest way to produce beef," that report says in its opening sentence. Later it advises sending us to the feedlot as young as possible ("directly into the feedlot at weaning"). That both uses the most grain and produces the highest profits.

We cattle and you men have had intertwined destinies for at least five thousand years. You have used us, and we have also used you—to bring me my hay all winter, for example. I don't say it has been an equal exchange; it hasn't. But as long as we can lead natural lives on farms, our part of the bargain is a fair one. And, as I have pointed out, in the twentieth century it's only as your livestock we would get to exist at all. We want to live.

What we don't want is to be condemned to feedlots. And that's my second plea to you. Help to free us. Of course beef will cost more—about ten percent more, according to the tables in Report 459—if we are allowed to live normally. But as vegetarians you are hardly going to be upset by that. Anyway, for that modest increase in cost, you'd not only be saving fellow creatures from needless suffering, you'd be doing three other good things. You'd be releasing literally millions of tons of grain a year. You'd be helping to keep American farms going. (Feedlots have nothing to do with farming. They are mostly owned by giant corporations, and they are pure agribusiness.) And finally you would be restoring some honorable jobs for human beings —working as what are known as cowboys in the West and as cowmen in the East. I should think even meat-eaters would be attracted by a program like that.

In ending, I can't resist setting straight a famous quotation from one of your philosophers. John Stuart Mill used to say that the true purpose of society is to produce the greatest happiness for the greatest number of human beings. It's a concept he got from Jeremy Bentham. But his saying didn't stop there, as a lot of you think it did. He added that as far as possible the principle should extend "to the whole sentient creation." And as for Bentham, *he* said that in deciding whose welfare to consider, "The question is not, can they reason? nor, can they speak? but, can they suffer?"

I think that includes my brothers out West.

Yours sincerely,
Michel du Bos

The Possibility Tax

JOHN TODHUNTER, now thirty-seven, is an associate professor of chemistry at the University of Colorado. He earns $24,000 a year, and has no outside income. Last year he paid $19,678 in federal income tax. Why so much? Because two years ago his IRS district completed a Potential Earnings Appraisal of all taxpayers in Colorado. After careful study of Professor Todhunter's case, a district assessor decided that he could easily earn $60,000 a year in private industry—and then keyed his tax liability to that figure. Although Todhunter likes teaching, and had meant to make it a lifetime career, he is about to take a job in the pesticide-development division of Allied Chemical.

Karen Bellevance, twenty-eight, is a social worker in Portsmouth, New Hampshire. She earns $18,000 a year. Last spring the IRS set *her* income tax at $52,000. Ms. Bellevance happens to be a strikingly beautiful woman with a magnificent figure, and the district assessor determined that if she became a prostitute in Boston, her earnings would be in the $100,000 range. This was no snap judgment, but a careful decision based on close examination. Furthermore, as the law requires in cases where the taxpayer files an appeal, his decision was subject to confirmation by outside authorities. Two Boston pimps confirmed his estimate in notarized affidavits.

Ms. Bellevance has not yet moved to Boston. Stubborn as well as beautiful, she is still doing social work in Portsmouth. To pay her taxes, she has borrowed money from her family. In addition, she works most evenings as a cocktail waitress—and she is a very good one. Tips included, she is picking up about $25,000 a year at the cocktail lounge, all of which she devotes to her quarterly tax payments.

Richard Hornig, twenty-three, is a second-year law student at Stanford. He ranks fourth in his class. Under a tax stabilization agreement he worked out with the IRS when he was seventeen and a freshman at Reed College, he pays only $100 a year in income tax. The agreement will lapse in two years, however, and the IRS has already told young Hornig that he can expect his tax liability to jump instantly to $11,000. A district assessor, having examined his law school record and personality index, has perceived a very attractive capability for personal claims work. Richard is, of course, under no obligation to enter that field. It's just that he will be taxed as if he were in it.

Richard's original hope was to start his career as a law clerk, preferably for an appellate judge. He now plans immediately to join a firm specializing in malpractice suits.

All this is fantasy as applied to people. Transform the people into land, however, and you have a fairly close analogy to how much of America's farmland and woodland are in fact taxed. There are numerous local exceptions; there are whole states that have made massive and even moderately successful attempts to ease the problem. But the fact remains that our prevailing doctrine of land taxation is that of "highest possible use," meaning most profitable possible use. "High" refers exclusively to the return the land can be made to pay, never mind how.

If you made the transformation for the three cases above, it would go something like this. (I don't pretend to perfect accuracy. Land-use law and tax law are both complicated, and every jurisdiction is different. But a mistake in detail here doesn't really matter. If what I say doesn't apply in that particular district, it is certain to in some other district nearby.)

Rancho Palaverde, 262 acres, is a dairy farm in eastern Colorado. The owner's net income last year, milking fifty-one Guernseys, was $24,000. Because the farm is less than two miles from a major new highway, it has become attractive though not prime development land—with maximum exploitation, worth several thousand an acre. It is consequently assessed at several thousand an acre, and the property tax has now climbed to $19,678. Obviously the owner must sell; the only choice he has in the matter is whether his farm will become a shopping center or a subdivision.

The old Bellevance place, 400 acres, is in a hilly region of New Hampshire. There are two brooks, a waterfall, and, from the higher land, views averaging thirty miles. Thousands of sugar maples, white birches, spruces, and beeches. Deer, raccoons, occasional wandering bears, and many smaller animals. Trout.

The owner inherited the place from his mother in 1957. It was then assessed at $16,000, and the annual tax ran around $225. It had been in the family for a century.

Twenty-five years later, the owner persists in regarding

the place as woodland. He occasionally cuts a few cords of firewood at the lower end, and still more occasionally allows selective logging over the whole tract—being careful to avoid erosion, spare the stream banks, and in general protect the beauty of the land, which he loves. His income from these two activities averages well under $1000 a year.

Because the land *is* so beautiful, and because it contains more than two hundred potential building sites with views, it has prime development potential. It is currently assessed at just over half a million. It has not yielded sufficient return to pay its taxes since 1968. At first the owner paid them out of his income from the family hardware store. As the tax steadily rose, he adopted a more desperate strategy. Now he sells off a couple of five-acre building lots every year or two. He nets just enough to keep paying his taxes.

Marshlands is a private wildlife refuge near a major western city. Much of it is shallow bog and meandering streams. Eight years ago, when heavy industry began to move in that direction, the owner made a tax-stabilization agreement with the county authorities. They like wild geese, too.

He is not going to be able to renew it, because other taxpayers in the county resent the low tax he is paying, and argue with some justice that they are subsidizing him. If he wants a wildlife refuge, they say, let him donate the land to the state—or sell it, if the state is willing to buy. Otherwise, let's fill the marsh in, zone the tract industrial, and start getting a decent tax return.

The whole issue is immensely complicated. No one would argue, least of all me, that taxes should be kept low on open land simply so that an owner, be he farmer, or nature-lover, or ordinary hard-eyed land speculator, can conveniently wait while the price rises, and then make a killing. Many would argue over the best way to prevent this, whether an immense capital gains tax if and when the land is sold for development, or the severing of development rights, or whatever. But one thing is crystal clear. If we continue to tax farmland, woodland, and marshland not on the basis of what they are worth as farmland, woodland, and marshland, but by figuring what they would be worth under conditions of maximum exploitation, one day we will look up and notice that we have maximally exploited our whole country. And unlike our ancestors, we won't be able to sail west and start over on some fresh new continent.

R. Brickman

Part IV

Nuclear Disobedience

THIS ESSAY IS GOING TO BE a little bit embarrassing in its present company, like a Jehovah's Witness who has strayed into an Episcopal picnic. He *will* preach. The Episcopalians may like what the fellow says, but he's too earnest for them: he keeps waving his arms and making the same point over and over, long after the entire audience has grasped it, committed it to memory, and possibly tried repeating it backwards in rhymed couplets. If only he'd sit down and eat a deviled egg, and stop all that shouting, they could get on with the day's activities.

As it happens, I am an Episcopalian myself, and very fond of picnics. Normally I would sympathize with the other essays and be on their side against this one. Even as it is, I won't blame them much if they crowd back along the page and glower. But for once I am constrained to play the sweating Witness.

What I have to witness is the familiar fact that the United States possesses weapons which are too powerful for it to control, and which may at any time destroy us and the world, without anyone's ever quite having meant to. We all know about our danger, and just as soon as our government and the Russian government (and, of course, the Chinese, French, and British governments) reach an agreement to disarm, we will all breathe a huge sigh of relief and maybe give up smoking. So we weren't to be extinguished after all.

Meanwhile, progress toward such an agreement is imperceptible, and the danger increases. What does any man do to avert it? Well, some write letters to newspapers, and some distribute leaflets. Some go to see their congressman, and urge that the United States should renounce its nuclear bombs now, whether Russia does or not. (The congressman, if he is typical, explains that this would be bad politics.) A few daring ones sail their boats into the test areas or picket missile bases, and they are ignored or quietly put in jail. Most of us wait with a mixture of hope and resignation for our government to do something, and pray that extinction doesn't come first. And while we wait, we help to increase the danger. As Air Force officers, we fly live bombs over the Arctic, and sometimes over the towns where our children lie sleeping. As physicists we design new and worse weapons. As technicians we build them. As administrators we plan them. As taxpayers we pay for them. And we don't know what else we can do. For surely if there were anything, our government would tell us, or the people would rise with a thunderous voice and tell the government.

The worst of it is that those of us who write the letters and plead with the congressmen actually have a feeling of virtue. We tell ourselves that we are doing all a single man can do, and if we die in a nuclear blast it won't be our fault. Some of us think in our heart of hearts that whatever happens to the others, we won't die in one—it would be too unfair. At the last minute, we secretly feel, some god will step out of the machine and rescue those of us who protested. Or at least one ought to.

Henry Thoreau, from whose essay "Civil Disobedience" I take my text, has something to say about this feeling. He was talking, a hundred and twelve years ago, about those Americans who knew in their souls that slavery was wrong and who wished to see it ended. "They hesitate and they regret," says Thoreau, "and sometimes they petition; but they do nothing in earnest and with effect. They will wait, well disposed, for others to remedy the evil, that they may no longer have it to regret. At most, they give only a cheap vote, and a feeble countenance and God-speed, to the right, as it goes by them." Such as these, says Thoreau, "command no more respect than men of straw or a lump of dirt." So much for our sense of virtue in that we wrote a letter or signed a petition. Men of flesh have to take stronger action than that.

There's another problem, of course, and Thoreau deals with that, too. It is hard for a single person *to* take much action, in a country like the United States. Solitary action seems undemocratic. As Thoreau puts it, "Men, generally, under such a government as this, think that they ought to wait until they have persuaded the majority. . . ." If a minority of us know that we must renounce nuclear weapons here and now, while we still can, and the majority hasn't realized it yet, then our job is to educate and persuade the majority. And how are we to do it, except with letters and petitions and television shows, and other harmless expressions of opinion?

On all expedient matters, Thoreau would agree with this view, and so must any good citizen. On matters of total conscience, such as slavery and the use of radiation, another and a harder rule applies. In matters of total conscience, men sometimes have to disobey the government and the half-felt will of the majority. Indeed, the disobedience of conscientious men may provide the only means through which the majority can find its true will. The thunderous voice of the people has its origin in the stubborn throats of just such men. Silence them, and there is no check left on government but the opinion poll, which is no check at all. Thoreau puts the case more succinctly. In matters of total conscience, he says, "Any man more right than his neighbors constitutes a majority of one already." As this special kind of majority, it is his plain duty to act.

What this means in the United States now, it seems to me, is that those who care whether humanity survives must begin to risk something more than their signatures on a petition. Those of us who fly live bombs could always try refusing. Those of us who build them could look for other work. Those of us who are reservists in the armed forces—and I am one myself—could serve notice that we will not fight in a nuclear war. (That very few of us would have a chance to fight—our chief role, like that of other people, being to perish—is for the moment beside the question. So is the fact that we seem just as likely to end our species in a peaceful accident as in war.) Those of us who finance this petard with which we are to hoist ourselves could even try not paying our taxes. It would be interesting to see what happened if two or three hundred thousand of us did refuse to pay next year.

There would be a special rightness in Americans doing these things. As much as anyone, we are responsible for letting the weapon out of control in the first place. Our technology and our genius built it; our money paid for it. We were the ones who took an atomic bomb which, in order to serve warning on Japan, we could perhaps have dropped in the open sea off Yokohama or into one of the great inland forests, and released its radiation onto a city full of human beings. Three days later, while the Japanese were deciding whether or not to surrender, we repeated the act on another city. Japanese are still dying of leukemia as a result. There is a chance that for the rest of history some Japanese babies will be monstrously mutated as a result. We did that.

That the Japanese would almost certainly have loosed radiation on our cities in 1945, if they had had the bombs, is no counter-argument. We are the ones who did do it, and in consequence we have a little more atomic responsibility than anyone else. Decent Germans must feel a special concern for Israel because of the Jews Germany slaughtered, and decent Israelis must be concerned for Palestine Arabs because of the land Israel has taken. Decent Americans must feel that concern for the whole human race, insofar as we have threatened its health and its survival with our free use of radiation. Possibly we had to do what we did in 1945. Possibly we have to be the ones to stop now. Even self-interest suggests that. After all, anyone who believes the Japanese would have used nuclear weapons on us in 1945, supposing they'd had them, must believe that some day the English, the French, the Russians, the Cubans, our surviving Indians *will* use them on us. Anyone who believes that and who does not push in earnest and with effect toward disarmament is a fool.

One more point needs to be brought up, and I want to beat the reader to it. The point is simply whether all this talk about extinction unless the world gives up nuclear weapons isn't rather alarmist. After all, we Episcopalians have been going on our picnics for years, and we haven't been washed out yet. People have always been claiming that the world was about to come to an end, unless this or that was done, and they have been wrong every single time. Our government assures us they are wrong this time—and would probably add that those who refuse to fly live bombs or pay their taxes will most assuredly go to jail.

I like to imagine a council of Blackfoot Indians about the year 1800. They are discussing a rumor that white men are slowly moving west, and that they have with them a terrible new weapon that shoots fire. Certain alarmists on the council predict disaster.

"Pooh," answer the rest. "People said that when the bow-and-arrow was invented. Remember when those other white men came up from Mexico on horses? We had never seen horses, and you hysterical types were running around moaning that all was lost. Remember, we told you we'd get our own horses and restore the balance of power? Well, didn't we? Don't be so excitable. You'll be predicting the end of buffalo next."

Ask the surviving Blackfoot Indians whether or not their world came to an end.

I also like to imagine an informal conclave of Neanderthal hunters about the year 74,000 B.C. They are discussing a new kind of flint spear used by the Cro-Magnons in the most recent fight. Certain alarmists among the hunters predict disaster.

"Pooh," answer the rest. "People said that when the throwing stick was invented. We'll get our own flint spears and restore the balance of power. Too dangerous? You'd rather make a treaty? Listen, we'd rather run a little risk than make a treaty with those damn Cro-Magnons. What do you want to do, compromise the Neanderthal way of life? You'll be predicting the end of mammoths next."

As the Neanderthals were entirely wiped out ("Evidence from Krapina in Croatia," wrote Professor Hooton of Harvard, "indicates in no uncertain terms that the Neanderthaloids in this region were eaten by their more highly evolved successors") . . . since Neanderthals are extinct, it is difficult to question them. But ask their ghosts whether or not their world came to an end.

The only difference now is that with radiation we can all die together, instead of some doing the wiping out and some the surviving. Or even if there should be survivors of the nuclear war or the nuclear mistake, what guarantee has anyone that America will be cast in the role of the Cro-Magnons?

It is very easy to assume that government—ours, the Russian, the World Court, any government—must be right. Government represents legitimacy, tradition, law and order, the sanction of things as they are. These are things to be respected. And yet hear Thoreau once more. "A common and natural result of an undue respect for law is, that you may see a file of soldiers, colonel, captain, corporal, privates, powder-monkeys and all, marching in admirable order over hill and dale to the wars, against their wills, ay, against their common sense and consciences, which makes it very steep marching indeed."

It would be nice to hear that those against whom we march were abandoning nuclear weapons of their own accord, without waiting for us. But suppose they don't? Suppose they need the example of the United States, which our government, busy marching over hill and dale, seems unable to give them.

If a few of us who know the peril do not step out of that file, even if it means losing our corporal's stripes, who will there be to head off the column from the cliff?

Postscript, 1983. The little essay you've just read is a genuine antique. I wrote it twenty-two years ago. It originally appeared as the final piece of my long-ago, long-forgotten first book. I haven't changed a word.

The terrifying thing is how timely it remains. Only two details are dated. No one is sailing into nuclear test areas these days, since the tests are all underground now. That's a gain for protestors, since there is less radioactive fallout. It's also a gain for the government, since an underground test is harder *to* protest, and also less conspicuous than devastating Bikini or Eniwetok, and hence less likely to alarm people. And the list of nuclear powers now goes well beyond the United States, Russia, England, France, and China. India, Israel, probably Pakistan, probably South Africa have come crashing into the club. There may be still more with a bomb or two.

Otherwise, things remain very much as they were in 1961. Politicians, ours and theirs, are still saying the same things. Eternally aimed nuclear weapons still point to Moscow and Washington, and probably hundreds or even thousands of other places as well. The danger of nuclear war has slowly but steadily risen, along with the number of weapons and powers. All of that is depressing.

And yet there is good news, too. World opinion is much more mobilized than it was in 1961. Back then, there was really no chance that people who understood the dangers could turn the course of things. There were too few of them, and they were too disorganized. Now there is a chance.

I can illustrate the change from my own life. Back in 1961, the only thing I could think to do for the sake of peace (besides write the essay) was to go on a "peace walk," one of the first ever held at Dartmouth College.

The walk was organized by an undergraduate named Anthony Graham-White and by a couple of faculty members. We were to walk five miles. From Webster Hall, on the edge of the Dartmouth green, down to White River Junction, Vermont. Despite a few banners and signs, we were not an impressive sight. In those days Dartmouth had about 3,000 students and 250 faculty members, not counting the medical school, engineering school, and business school. Even though it was a beautiful mild day, a bare fifty people gathered for the walk—and some of those were neither faculty nor student, but townspeople. One was my infant daughter, in a baby carriage.

We were not the only group in front of Webster Hall. Peace walks, at least in those days, brought out war supporters, too. About twenty members of the Dartmouth chapter of Young Americans for Freedom were circling around us, waving *their* signs. The one that made a lasting impression on me was a big piece of yellow cardboard, with a rather good sketch of a mushroom cloud on it, and the caption "Keep America Safe." I wondered if the student artist who drew it realized it would work as well for our side as his.

We watched the Young Americans, and they watched us; nobody else paid much attention at all. Two fraternities were having a baseball game on the green, and a couple of hundred students were watching that, with maybe one bored glance at the milling little groups in front of Webster Hall. At the time, that infuriated me. I thought, "That's why we'll *have* a nuclear war. Except for a little group of fanatics who started it, and another little group of fanatics who tried in vain to prevent it, everyone was watching baseball."

With twenty years of perspective, I see the matter differently, see that apathy is by no means always bad. If everyone were "involved" or "concerned" all the time, the insanity rate would be up around 80 percent. There are so many causes and needs and injustices in the world that to let oneself care about even all the urgent ones would lead most of us to instant emotional bankruptcy.

All the same, averting nuclear war is a special case, since practically all other causes will cease to exist if we do have one. There may be survivors, but there certainly is not going to be much concern, the year after the war, over which party controls the Senate, or whether school instruction in New York should be bilingual, or how to raise money for the Los Angeles Philharmonic, or what progress is being made in curing cerebral palsy.

For that reason I rejoice at how much more involved people at Dartmouth are now. Last year, so many students and faculty went to New York for the great anti-nuclear rally that Vermont Transit ran out of buses. (And couldn't borrow any from other New England bus lines, because they had all run out, too.) This year there is an official part of the college, complete with office and staff support, called the Program for Education on the Threat of Nuclear War. It is the only program we have that's devoted to a single issue, and also the only one that in its name takes a position.

The other programs are all called things like Policy Studies and Women's Studies and Environmental Studies. No one even considered calling this one Nuclear Studies, still less the Program for Education on the Threats and Blessings of Nuclear War.

Similarly, the only stand I'm aware of that the trustees have ever taken on a public matter was their statement in April, 1982, urging both the college and the country to learn more about nuclear perils.

These are encouraging signs, and they are to be found everywhere. In 1961, little Vermont towns, far from any college, considered it their business at town meeting to mind the town's business. By 1981, some of them felt differently. Eighteen voted, along with setting a highway budget and electing someone to be selectman, to request the federal government to cease both the testing and the production of nuclear weapons. That's only a tiny fraction of the 246 towns in the state; it was also only a tiny hint of what was to come. In 1982, another 161 towns passed the same resolution. In West Windsor it passed by unanimous voice vote—and then the whole town meeting rose and sang "America."

But the best news is that in 1983 there is good solid organization for the kind of resistance it will take to move politicians and generals. Non-binding votes in little Vermont towns certainly aren't going to. Or even non-binding votes in big states.

Back in 1961, I wistfully speculated on tax resistance. "It would be interesting to see what happened if two or three hundred thousand of us did refuse to pay next year," I wrote—and of course went on to pay my 1962 income tax, telephone excise tax, gasoline tax, etc. Apart from all other considerations, it is a scary thing to start refusing to pay taxes all by oneself. There were no fellow refusers to give me courage—or if there were I didn't know about them.

Vietnam has happened since then, and there is now a large group of Americans trained in what might be called loyal disobedience. Maybe even patriotic disobedience. Some of that training was in refusal to pay taxes. It really isn't all that scary once you get into it. In 1983 there is an organization, to which I belong, whose members have all signed a pledge to begin weapons-tax refusal as soon as the membership reaches 100,000. (It's called Conscience & Military Tax Campaign, and its headquarters is at 44 Bellhaven Road, Bellport, New York 11713.)

The threat of nuclear war has clearly increased since 1961. But the will to resist preparations for the war has clearly increased even more. I think it is in the process of becoming a national movement. Farms and farmers may survive yet, along with symphony orchestras and medical research. That would be nice.